W9-BHZ-565

Lou Jacobs, Jr.

Instant
Photography

illustrated with photographs

Lothrop, Lee & Shepard Company

A Division of William Morrow & Company, Inc.
New York

770.28
JAC
B&T
2-77
5.61

Also by Lou Jacobs, Jr.

YOU AND YOUR CAMERA

Photo Credits
Polaroid Corporation: pages 4, 6, 8, 9, 11, 17, 19, 20, 21, 24, 25, 26, 27, 29, 42, 50 bottom, 51, 52, 53, 56, 60, 67, 78, 91, 97 right, 99, 105, 107, 108, 109, 112 top, 117, 126.
Keystone Division of Berkey Photo, Inc.: pages 22 top, 31.
Kalimar, Inc.: pages 112 bottom, 114.
All other photographs by the author except where noted.

Copyright © 1976 by Lou Jacobs, Jr.
All rights reserved. No part of this book may be reproduced or utilized in any form or by any means, electronic or mechanical, including photocopying, recording or by any information storage and retrieval system, without permission in writing from the Publisher. Inquiries should be addressed to Lothrop, Lee & Shepard Company, 105 Madison Ave., New York, N. Y. 10016.

Printed in the United States of America.

1 2 3 4 5 80 79 78 77 76

Library of Congress Cataloging in Publication Data

Jacobs, Lou.
  Instant photography.
  Bibliography: p.
  1. Polaroid Land camera—Juvenile literature.
2. Photography—Juvenile literature. I. Title.
TR263.P6J3   770'.28   75-42438
ISBN 0-688-41741-8
ISBN 0-688-51741-2 lib. bdg.

Contents

Foreword

This is the first book for young photographers devoted exclusively to the skills, equipment, and materials for instant photography. Most people take pictures for fun, or to have a record of something or someone, and the instant process can result in high-quality photographs.

I first used a Polaroid Land camera in 1955, and have owned or used more than a dozen different models since then. I was privileged to experiment with Polacolor film before it was introduced for sale in the early 1960s, and I have worked closely with the Polaroid Corporation as new products were developed. As a professional photographer, writer, and teacher for more than twenty-five years, I have a high regard for instant photography. It helps us see, interpret, record, and learn through the world's most popular hobby.

Many of the illustrations in this book were taken during past years as I used instant cameras and films for fun and profit. In addition, photographs and up-to-date technical information were made available to me by Jean Anwyll, Don Dery, and Eleanor Howison of the Polaroid Corporation, and I am grateful for their help.

What is Instant Photography?

After you take a picture with a conventional camera, there's a waiting period of several days or a week, unless you process your own films. During the time it takes pictures to be developed and returned to you, it's easy to forget what you took, and you can get very impatient to see how your photographs came out.

Instant photography eliminates the middle man and all the delays. In one minute or less after snapping the shutter of an instant camera, you have a finished print in black and white or color, or you may be watching a color print develop. Instant films and cameras are chemical and mechanical wonders offering all sorts of advantages to photographers.

A Bit of History

For decades after the invention of photography in the 1830s, it was a terribly slow process compared to what we know today. During the Civil War, for instance, Matthew Brady and his crew had to make their exposures on glass plates while the sensitized coating was still wet. These men worked out of horse-drawn "darkrooms" moved from place to place on the battlefields, because their pictures also had to be developed before the coating dried. That was "instant" photography the hard way!

7

In the 1880s George Eastman perfected photographic film in rolls. One loading of his early Kodak was enough for 100 pictures, after which the whole camera was sent to the factory; the film was developed and a new roll was loaded before the camera was returned to the owner.

After World War II, the photographic industry in the United States and abroad began to grow quickly. All sorts of fantastic new cameras, lenses, films, and other equipment are available now. However, until instant photography was invented, films had to be developed by the photographer or by a processing lab where prints are also made. In 1948 Dr. Edwin H. Land reduced the developing and printing time to seconds when he introduced the instant picture process from the Polaroid Corporation.

Dr. Edwin Land, inventor of the instant photography process.

This 1948 Model 95 was the first instant camera.
Everything about it worked more slowly than
present-day models.

Some years before "pictures in a minute" were on the market, Dr. Land was experimenting in chemistry and physics as a Harvard student. In 1943, when his young daughter asked how long she would have to wait to see some snapshots he had taken, Land began wondering how photographs might be developed as prints right inside the camera. In his own small laboratory he set to work finding an answer.

By 1947 Dr. Land was able to announce the first Polaroid Land camera, which went on sale the next year. Called the Model 95, it weighed nearly four pounds, produced sepia-toned prints of varying quality in one minute, and sold for $89.95.

9

Since that time, there have been dozens of instant cameras, each one offering improvements over older models. Instead of roll films that develop inside the camera, there are now pack films that develop outside the camera. In 1960 the Model 900 Electric Eye, the J33, and the J66 were the first Land cameras with automatic "electric eye" exposure systems. Now all instant cameras except one are automatic; you make a few simple settings, point the camera, and shoot. The electric eye system usually assures a well-exposed print.

Until 1963 all instant prints were black and white. At that time full color pictures in a minute made instant photography even more exciting. Since then Polacolor film has been improved, and the pictures are brighter. Even more important, there are now several instant camera models that sell for around $20.00 complete with automatic exposure, provisions for flash, and sharp lenses. In the next chapter, all available cameras are described.

The highlight of instant camera history is a radically different camera called the SX-70. Prints from other instant cameras are timed during development, and then peeled away from a negative which is discarded. SX-70 pictures are plastic-coated, and develop while you watch. How this happens is described in the next chapter.

In only three decades instant photography has become easier and faster with improved quality. Today amateurs and professionals alike shoot pictures they can enjoy seconds later.

Advantages of Instant Photography

Whether you are just learning photography or already have some experience with cameras, the greatest advantage of instant picture-taking is being able to see your prints immediately. An artist can erase pencil lines or paint over

Often an instant camera allows you to share the fun of pictures while something is actually happening.

the forms on a canvas, but with conventional cameras, you must shoot plenty of variations of a scene, because you cannot make changes on prints or slides. By the time your pictures are processed, you and your subjects are usually parted, and it may be difficult or impossible to shoot them again.

Reshooting to "erase" or correct mistakes on the spot is built into instant photography. If the subject's expression, the exposure, the camera angle, the composition, or your timing is not satisfactory in a print, you can make the necessary changes and try again a minute later. Almost every mistake that bothers a beginner can be corrected before the opportunity has vanished. You can:

- sharpen the focus and steady the camera (sometimes by mounting it on a tripod) if your prints are fuzzy;
- ask someone to smile or turn where the lighting is better;
- find a less distracting background or shift the camera for a better composition;
- add flash if the existing light is too weak;
- shoot action again if you missed an exciting moment.

11

With an instant camera you can learn photography more quickly and have fun doing it. Your confidence increases as you see your pictures improving right away, and you are ready to try new things. It's also great to have other people admire your prints just moments after they are shot. Once you learn good technique, you won't forget it, any more than you can forget how to write a letter or fly a kite. Later, if you turn to a conventional camera that offers more lenses and faster operation, everything you learned from instant photography will be useful for shooting better pictures.

A Few More Facts

- Duplicate instant prints can be made in two ways. Either shoot a similar or identical picture immediately to give away or save, or send the original picture to the Polaroid Copy Service nearest your home, in Cambridge, Massachusetts or El Segundo, California. In a matter of days you will receive excellent copies or enlargements; color slides can even be made from your color prints.
- Even the least expensive instant cameras can take pictures in fairly dim light without flash, using fast black and white instant film.
- Flashcubes, bulbs, or attachments are made for all instant cameras; two Keystone 60-Second models have built-in electronic flash.
- Accessories for portraits and close-ups, and self-timers that allow you to get into your own pictures, are available for many models.
- A Polaroid print in color or black and white may cost a few cents more than a conventional print, but this is easily balanced by the convenience of seeing your pictures immediately. Enlargements are similar in price to those made from conventional negatives, and

may even cost less, depending on local rates. In addition, while processing and print quality from conventional labs varies greatly, copies and enlargements from Polaroid Copy Service are consistently good.
- The Polaroid Corporation has Service Centers in the United States and Europe where cameras are repaired quickly. There is also a hotline telephone directly to their headquarters for answers to problems with a camera or film. See page 124.

People are always pleased with a really good photo of themselves, or of you, or of a memorable place or event. An instant photograph is also the world's best "ice-breaker." Strangers become acquaintances as soon as you hand over an instant print. A mechanic in a rural French town once repaired my car on a Sunday just after I shot a few instant pictures of him.

Taking pictures is a wonderful way to record, to communicate, and especially, to express yourself. Take your instant camera seriously, and it can be a marvelous medium for seeing—and showing—the world around you. Dr. Land once said, "Photography can teach people to look, to feel, to remember in a way that they didn't know they could." Instant photography does it all sooner.

This French farm family was looking at its first instant print in 1955. Many people are still amazed to see themselves in seconds.

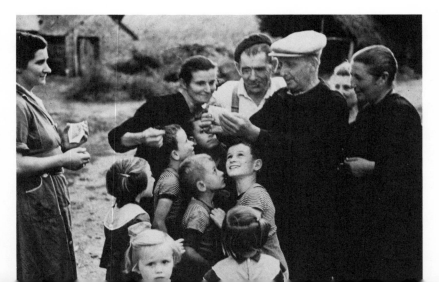

Instant Cameras and Films: How They Work

Knowing how an instant camera works and what happens to the film when you expose it can help you take better pictures. You don't have to be an engineer or scientist, but the basic facts will give you more technical confidence, and may be a stepping stone to creativity.

How Instant Pack Cameras Work

Instant pack cameras are similar to conventional models in many ways, and they are discussed below. SX-70 models, using a different type of film, are described later in this chapter.

The camera body: This is simply a light-tight box with a lens at one end and film inside the box opposite the lens. Some instant camera models are made of molded plastic, and others are made of metal and plastic with a bellows that extends out when the camera is open and folds flat when it is closed.

When the back of an instant camera is unlatched, it swings open to allow a pack of film to fit neatly inside. At one end of the hinged back are a pair of stainless steel rollers that must be kept clean. Within the body is a cavity for batteries that power the automatic exposure system; these must be replaced at least once a year.

The camera lens: This is the "eye" of the camera

The open back of the Super Shooter is typical of instant cameras. Rollers at left must be kept clean and batteries inside replaced once a year.

through which light rays pass to form an image on the film. A lens consists of several pieces of specially ground glass or molded plastic, carefully designed and assembled for a specific camera.

Behind the lens is either a series of holes in a metal disk or a mechanism made of overlapping metal leaves called a *diaphragm.* These openings, along with the *shutter speed,* regulate the amount of light that reaches the film. Openings in a disk or diaphragm (depending on the camera model) are called *f-stops,* and they have numerical ratings that are common to all cameras. The lower the f-stop number, such as f/2, f/3.5, or f/4.5, the larger the opening. Many instant cameras have a maximum opening of about f/8, and a minimum one of f/64 or f/96. You should be familiar with f-stops in order to compare lenses and cameras; however, since instant cameras expose automatically, you need not worry about f-stops when taking pictures. The only exception is the Polaroid Model 195 camera. It has an f/4.5 lens and conventional f-stop settings because it is not automatic.

F-stops are also involved in a photographic principle called *depth of field.* This term refers to the area of a scene that appears in sharp focus from the closest to the farthest object or person, and is explained fully in Chapter 7.

The camera shutter: The shutter is the part of the camera that opens and closes very rapidly when you press the button. This allows light to reach the film.

Instant cameras have either mechanical or electronic shutters. A mechanical shutter has a limited number of speeds with which to take pictures. An electronic shutter operates through a wide range of speeds from a second or two to 1/500 or 1/600 second, depending on the camera model.

Photography is more fun when you understand how an instant camera works and practice using it under various conditions.

The Model 195 is the "thinking person's camera" because it's not automatic. It can be used with all three film types shown.

Except for the Polaroid Model 195, instant cameras do not allow you to choose your shutter speed, because it is selected by the automatic exposure system. In bright sun or on a bright cloudy day, the electric eye system automatically chooses faster shutter speeds which help to "freeze" action on instant prints.

In most indoor situations and outdoors when there is no direct sunlight, many instant cameras with electronic shutters can be used to take pictures without flash. However, keep in mind that the shutter speeds selected by the automatic exposure system in these situations are usually very slow. It is difficult to hold a camera steadily under such circumstances, and blurred prints are often the result. To assure sharp pictures in dim light, either steady the camera on a firm base or tripod, or use flash.

Following is a chart of instant cameras for comparison of lens openings and shutter speeds. Though you do not adjust these settings directly (except for the Model 195), you should be familiar with the capabilities of the camera you use.

17

CAMERA	MAXIMUM AND MINIMUM LENS OPENINGS	SHUTTER SPEEDS
Polaroid Model 420	f/8.8 to f/60	1 second to 1/600 second
Polaroid Model 430	f/8.8 to f/60	1 second to 1/600 second
Polaroid Model 440 Polaroid Model 450	f/8.8 to f/60	20 seconds to 1/600 second with film Types 105 and 108; 5 seconds to 1/600 second with film Type 107
Polaroid Model 195	f/3.8 to f/64	B*, 1 second to 1/500 second
Polaroid Super Shooter	f/8 to f/64	2 seconds to 1/500 second
Polaroid Zip	f/17.5 to f/90	1/200 second
Polaroid Electric Zip	f/8.8 to f/60	1/2 second to 1/500 second
Keystone Model 750	f/8.8 to f/45	10 seconds to 1/500 second
Keystone Model 800	f/8 to f/22	10 seconds to 1/500 second
Keystone Model 850	f/8 to f/22	10 seconds to 1/500 second

*B is the setting for time exposures; the shutter remains open as long as the button is depressed.

The least expensive of the Polaroid line are the Zip and the newer Electric Zip.

The camera viewfinder: The Zip, the Electric Zip, the Super Shooter, and Keystone cameras have window view-finders built into the camera body. Most other instant cameras have fold-up finders that hinge down to close the case compactly. It's a good idea to test your camera viewfinder carefully, especially if you wear glasses, to find out how accurately it frames a scene or portrait.

The Super Shooter uses all types of color and black and white films.

Focusing the camera: By setting a *distance scale* according to the number of feet from the camera to the subject, you focus the lens of a camera to produce a sharp image. Cameras with window viewfinders are focused by turning the lens to a footage mark that you estimate to be correct. In bright sun, the lens compensates for small errors, but in dim light you must be more accurate. For focusing on distant subjects (more than fifteen feet away), your guess need be less exact than for focusing on close subjects (from three or four feet to about eight feet), when only a precise setting assures sharpness. Practice measuring with a tape after setting the focus by guess, and your technique will improve.

Cameras with folding viewfinders focus by means of a *rangefinder*. Beside the viewfinder window is the rangefinder viewer through which two small images are seen. As you focus the lens (by shifting the front of the camera back and forth), one of the two small images shifts. When the two images merge into one, the camera lens is focused on your target. Until the images merge, the subject is out of focus. A rangefinder is more accurate and faster than

Focusing through a rangefinder: if the image is double (left), picture is out of focus; when images come together (right), lens is focused properly.

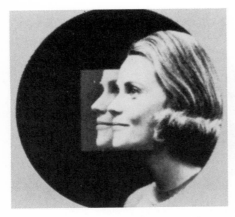 

OUT OF FOCUS   **IN FOCUS**

guesswork, but instant cameras with this feature cost more than those without it.

Flash connections: Flash is easy with all instant cameras, because the connections between flash source and shutter are built in, and exposure is automatically correct if your focus is accurate. Chapter 4 explains all about it.

The Super Shooter and both Zip models include a socket for flashcubes or bulbs, plus a transparent shield that folds out in front. The Polaroid 400 series cameras have a slot into which a Focused Flash cube holder can be connected. The Keystone 60-Second Rapid-Shot has a receptacle for a Ten-shot Flashbar, and Keystone Everflash cameras include built-in flash units. There's an accessory shoe on top of the Polaroid Model 195 for compact standard flashguns and electronic flash units. Instruction booklets for each camera make the use of these flash connections very clear.

It is important to read the booklet for your camera thoroughly. It offers a wealth of valuable information, not all of which can be repeated in this book. If you have no booklet, the Polaroid Corporation or Keystone will send a replacement. Their addresses are given on page 124.

This is the Model 450 Land camera shown with Focused Flash attachment and typical print.

The Keystone Everflash Model 850 (now discontinued) has built-in electronic flash and uses square or rectangular film packs.

Timers: Several instant cameras have built-in timers for print development. You can also buy an accessory timer and attach it to a camera neck strap. Of course, you can always refer to a watch or clock, but be precise to save film and frustration.

The timer on the Model 195 Land camera is typical of built-in print timers.

Understanding Automatic Exposure

An instant camera is really an ingeniously designed instrument. Next to the lens of most models is a small round opening for the electric eye sensor, except for the Zip which has a photometer window above the lens, and the Model 195 which has no electric eye. Light passes through the sensor opening and strikes a small battery-powered cell inside the camera which measures the intensity of the light. This information flows electronically to the camera's lens and shutter mechanisms, which are then automatically set for the correct exposure. In addition to the brightness of the light, the speed of your film influences properly exposed prints; a selector switch is set according to the film you are using.

While an electric eye system is fast and convenient, it can be "fooled." When you shoot into bright light, or if the light and dark contrast range of a scene is higher than average, a print may be too light or too dark. In such a case, you can adjust a lighten/darken ring around the camera lens (or a knob on the Zip) to correct and improve print exposure. With a little practice, you will discover how much to adjust the lighten/darken control for more consistently bright, clear prints.

How Instant Pack Films Work

A conventional negative film, either black and white or color, is exposed within a camera, removed, developed, and printed. An instant film is unique in that all these steps take place in seconds. Besides good camera operating techniques, the photographer need only be concerned with timing and the temperature of the air.

An instant pack film includes eight negative/positive sheets stacked within a metal frame. After you load a pack into the camera and close the back, you pull a paper tab sticking out of the end. This removes a long sheet of paper which serves as a light shield before the film is ready to use.

The following diagrams show what happens before, during, and after instant film is exposed.

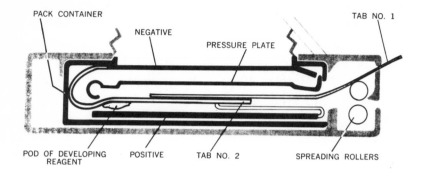

1. An instant negative is made of paper (except for Type 105 film described later). In this cross-section view, showing only one film in position, the negative on top faces the lens. It is exposed when you click the shutter. The pressure plate holds the negative flat to assure a sharp image when the lens is properly focused. Under the pressure plate is the positive portion of the film, which will become an instant print. It is *not* exposed in the camera.

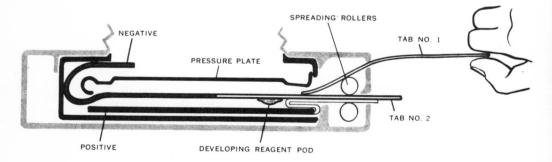

2. A pod of chemicals is attached to a paper tab (#2), while a smaller paper tab (#1) protrudes through a slot at the end of the camera. After the picture is taken, tab #1 is pulled, drawing the negative behind the pressure

plate, facing the future positive print but not yet touching it. At the same time, tab #2 is fed through a pair of stainless steel rollers, and appears outside the camera. Though it is not shown, a new negative comes into position for the next picture.

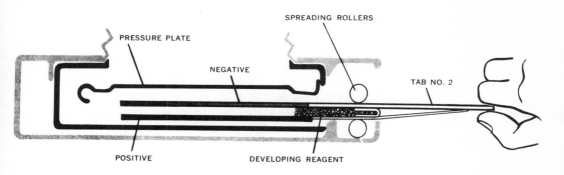

3. Tab #2 is now pulled in a steady movement at moderate speed, during which the pod of chemicals breaks open as it passes through the rollers. A jellied mixture of chemicals (also called a reagent) is spread evenly between the negative and positive as they come through the rollers and are pulled outside of the camera. By chemical means the image is transferred from the negative to the positive print. Development of the instant print is now timed for an interval that depends on the type of film and on the air temperature. Instructions come with each pack of film; I refer to them all the time, because I use several types of film and don't want to get mixed up.

4. Both the negative and positive have an opaque backing to prevent light from reaching them while they develop. When timing is complete, the finished print is peeled away from the paper negative. The print is now stabilized; this means it is no longer sensitive to light. The negative is discarded, except when you use Type 105 film. Some black and white prints must be preserved and protected by spreading another chemical over them from a print coater

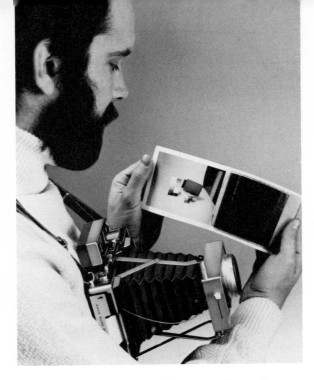

*The finished print is peeled away from the
negative after timing is complete.*

that comes with each film pack. However, the latest black
and white films do not require coating, and these will eventually replace the others. Color prints need not be coated,
but are slightly tacky when first peeled from the negative;
they dry in a few minutes.

Inside Polacolor films: Instant color film images are
formed through a combination of dyes and developers
linked together in a new type of molecule. A very complex
chemical procedure makes possible pictures with all the
hues of the rainbow. A well-exposed, properly developed
Polacolor print should be equal in quality to conventional
prints made by a good processing lab.

SX-70 Cameras and Film

The SX-70 is a new breed of instant camera, completely
unlike other instant cameras. With two of the four models

The Deluxe SX-70 Land camera opens for through-the-lens viewing and focusing.

you view and focus *through the lens.* This is called a *reflex* system, used in many popular 35mm and 2¼x2¼ conventional cameras. Within the SX-70 is a maze of transistors and wires that operate exposure automation, mirrors, and flash. The largest opening of the lens is f/8, and it can close down to the tiny opening of f/96 to make extremely close flash shots possible; the lens can be focused as close as ten inches with no attachments.

The electronic shutter of the SX-70 has speeds ranging from 1/18 second to 1/180 second, and will automatically time exposures as long as fourteen seconds. The camera includes a tiny electric motor which ejects prints immediately after exposure, as fast as you can press the shutter button, so you can shoot all ten color pictures in an SX-70 film pack in quick succession. Flash pictures are also automatically exposed with a ten-shot Flashbar attached into a slot above the SX-70 lens (details in Chapter 4).

While the DeLuxe and Model 2 SX-70s are reflex cameras, the Model 3 and the Pronto use a conventional viewfinder and a distance scale which is manually adjusted for correct focus. The first three SX-70s have f/8 lenses, and the Pronto uses an f/9.4 lens. All four models have automatic exposure controls and electric motors to eject exposed prints.

Here is how the ingenious SX-70 DeLuxe and Models 2 and 3 work.

1. The camera folds flat when not in use, and opens into the cross-section shape shown on page 29.

2. The image coming through the lens strikes an angled mirror, is reflected downward to another mirror, and up again, out through a small exit hole. Here a specially curved mirror reflects the image into the eyepiece of the viewfinder, precisely as the film will "see" it. As you focus the lens, the viewfinder image changes accordingly.

3. When the shutter button is depressed, the bottom mirror rises up against the top of the camera, bringing another mirror into place to reflect the image downward onto a now uncovered sheet of film.

4. After exposure, the double mirror drops back to shield the remaining film. At the same time, the film is motor-driven through two rollers which break a double pod of chemicals; these are then spread between the film's positive and negative layers. The development process continues outside the camera as you watch the picture you just shot appear.

The Pronto: This is the lightest version of the SX-70, weighing only 16 ounces. Its electronic system is able to combine flash and outdoor illumination to lighten shadows in bright sun. Shutter speeds range from one second to 1/125 second, and closest focus is three feet. The camera does not fold, but has many advantages of the more expensive models for a modest price.

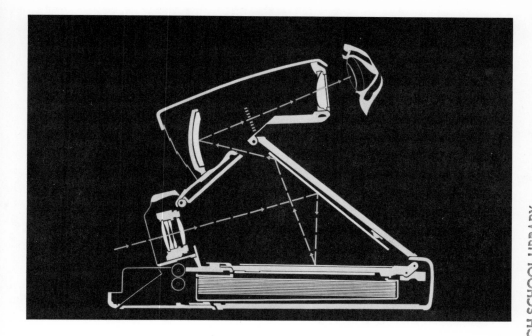

Top: *The image enters the lens and is reflected by a mirror system into the viewfinder.* Bottom: *As the exposure is made, the bottom mirror lifts up against the back to reflect the image downward onto SX-70 film. After exposure, the mirror drops back to viewing position.*

MONROVIA HIGH SCHOOL LIBRARY
MONROVIA, INDIANA 46157

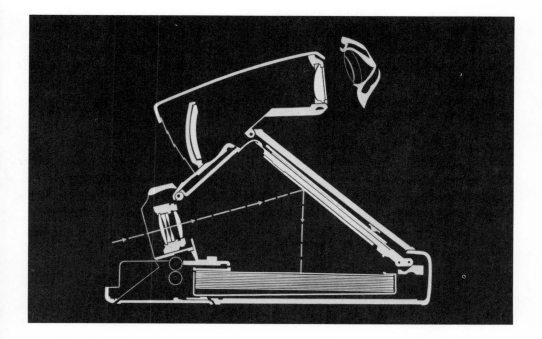

The Pronto includes the electronic exposure system of the SX-70 plus electric motor, and costs less.

SX-70 film: In order to create an instant film with nothing to throw away after development, a team of twenty-five Polaroid chemists worked for four years to produce a new film that would be self-processing outside the camera, and yet be unaffected by light after exposure. This was accomplished by including a combination of chemicals called an "opacifier" that blocks out light rays while the image develops. SX-70 film also contains many extremely thin layers of dyes, and the whole print is plastic-coated to prevent smudges of any kind. When a Polaroid representative demonstrated the SX-70 for me, she threw a print into a swimming pool moments after it came from the camera. Since it was waterproof, it was not damaged.

At first an SX-70 print looks like a cloudy turquoise-tinted square that is often slightly streaked. Within thirty seconds the streaks disappear and the image can be seen faintly. In five minutes the print is about 90 percent developed, and in ten minutes the full range of colors is complete. Dyes used in SX-70 film are very stable, though they will fade if exposed to sunlight for a long time, and the same dyes are used in Polacolor 2 pack film as a result of SX-70 research.

Types of Instant Cameras

Polaroid cameras: Of the eight listed on page 18, both Zips and the Super Shooter are relatively inexpensive, and yet versatile. The Zip uses only square black and white film, while the Electric Zip makes square color and black and white pictures, and the Super Shooter will accept all instant films, square and rectangular.

As the model numbers in the 400 series get higher, the cameras increase in price. More expensive cameras offer additional controls for focusing and exposure without flash. The Model 195 is the most professional instant camera with the largest lens, which means you can take pictures in dim light more easily without flash. The Model 195 requires the use of a separate exposure meter because it is not automatic.

While no manual adjustments are necessary with other automatic instant cameras (except for lighten/darken control), you must turn a small knob on the Zip to obtain proper exposure. Within the viewfinder window there is a tiny checkerboard grid at the bottom. When the exposure knob is rotated and there is enough light, the word "YES" is spelled out in the grid pattern. If "YES" does not appear, the light is too dim, and you must use flash. The Electric Zip has an automatic shutter, and the "YES" signal is not used.

Keystone instant cameras: Three models are available that use Polaroid pack films, and operate automatically in a fashion similar to Polaroid Land cameras. The Model 750 uses a ten-shot Flashbar, while Models 800 and 850 have built-in electronic flash units. These cameras are no longer manufactured, but many dealers may still have them for sale.

The Wizard XF 1000 made by Keystone uses SX-70 film packs. It is designed along the lines of the SX-70 Model 3, but it does not fold flat. Compare their features if this type of instant color photography has advantages for you.

Older instant cameras: Though only current models are described fully in this chapter, there are many older instant cameras that still may work very well. For instance, the Colorpack II and the Swinger from Polaroid are much like the Electric Zip and the Super Shooter in operation. The 400 series of cameras evolved from the 100, 200, and 300 series, all of which make fine pictures if the camera is in good working order. The Polaroid Model 360 had an electronic flash designed for use with it, and the Model 100 was a favorite of mine for many years.

Other older models include the Big Shot which takes only close portraits, and the Square Shooter that uses only square film (Type 88). The Polaroid Model 180 is much like the present Model 195. Both have a conventional shutter, and because they are not automated, I've often referred to them as "the thinking person's" cameras. Both the 180 and 195 have superior lenses, but are not as fast to use as electric eye models.

Instant roll film cameras of any age are still useful if they are in good condition, and black and white films are still made for them. The Model 80 is smaller than others, while the Models 850, 900, J-66, and J-33 include electric eye exposure control. With their non-automatic shutters and larger lenses, the Polaroid Models 110 and 110B can also be useful cameras. They were the "thinking person's" cameras of their day.

Types of Instant Pack Films

The following all make prints measuring 3¼ by 4¼ inches:

Polacolor 2 Type 108: This is similar to the original Colorpack film, but the colors are more brilliant, and images appear slightly sharper. This film is also for daylight, blue bulbs, and electronic flash. If you expose them by artificial light, meaning ordinary room lights or floodlights, both Type 108 films become warm and reddish. This is normal because of their color chemistry; you may experiment with correction filters such as the 80A or 80B in artificial light, but results are not ideal. Shoot from a tripod or steady base when using a filter, since it decreases the speed, or light sensitivity, of the film.

Type 107: This film is so fast, or light sensitive, that instant cameras can take pictures in dim light that are not possible with conventional cameras in the same price range. A conventional black and white film such as Tri-X has a speed rating of 400, while Type 107 is rated at 3,000. In bright sunlight this means the f-stop of an instant camera can be relatively small, thereby increasing the area of sharp focus, or depth of field. This is explained further in the next chapter.

I've taken very acceptable indoor shots with a Super Shooter and Type 107 film without flash. This film provides excellent tone quality from which fine copies and enlargements can be made.

Type 105: With a speed rating of 75 (the same as Polacolor), this film gives you a black and white print plus a fully developed negative, all in 30 seconds without a darkroom. As soon as the print is peeled away, the negative is immune to light, and can later be enlarged with sharpness and tonality equal to any conventional film. The negative must be soaked for a few minutes in a mild chemical solution, so its gummy coating will fall away. Polaroid makes a portable tank for this process. Then the negative can be hung to dry for half an hour. Users of Type 105 film are able to view their prints on the spot, and later improve composition and manipulate tone values when enlargements are made. If you have access to a darkroom, or wish to have prints made by a commercial lab, using Type 105 adds one more advantage to instant photography.

The following two films make prints 3¼ by 3⅜ inches:

Type 88: This is Polacolor film with exactly the same qualities as Type 108 described above. It is used in the Electric Zip, the Super Shooter, Square Shooter cameras, and several Keystone models.

Type 87: This is the same 3,000-speed film as Type 107, and is the only film used in the Zip camera, but it fits other models that take black and white square pictures. It need not be coated after development. This film and Type 88 make instant pictures less costly.

Roll films

The following are available for older instant cameras:
- Type 42 black and white film (speed rating is 200);
- Type 32 black and white film (speed rating is 400);
- Type 47 black and white film (speed rating is 3,000);
- Type 146-L high contrast black and white film which makes positive transparencies for projection (speed rating is 100).

Special-size films

Though you probably will not use them, the following are color and black and white Polaroid films made for 4x5 cameras:
- Type 58 Polacolor film, ten film packets to a box (speed rating is 75);
- Type 52 black and white film (speed rating is 400);

- Type 55 P/N black and white film which produces a usable negative and print in twenty seconds (speed rating is 50);
- Type 57 black and white film (speed rating is 3,000).

Film is available for nearly every Polaroid camera ever made since 1948. However, some older models cannot be used with Type 47 film because they are not sufficiently light-tight. You can call Polaroid's Customer Service toll-free number for information about the usefulness of an old roll film camera (see page 124).

Equipment and materials for instant photography are varied to cope with almost every picture situation you will meet. Let's go out now and take some pictures.

Shooting by Daylight

Before reading this chapter, I suggest you take some pictures with an instant camera because:
- you get the *feel* of a camera as you see your actual pictures;
- it takes a little while to fit your eye comfortably to the viewfinder and to learn to hold the camera steadily;
- experience in focusing and making adjustments for slight changes with the lighten/darken control is also valuable;
- you can gain as much from your personal picture-taking mistakes as you can from reading books.

Checklist for Better Pictures
- Be certain your camera is set to the correct film speed, because this guides the automation.
- Lens and finder should be spotless. Special lens cleaning tissues and solutions are available at camera shops. Handkerchiefs and facial tissues may make tiny scratches on a lens, so avoid them.
- Hold the camera without being tense, and brace your elbows against your sides. *Squeeze* the shutter release button. Don't jerk it. Make this your slogan: *Squeezing Saves Shots.*
- Practice guessing the distance between your camera

In sunlight all instant films are capable of sharp pictures with good tones and colors. This was taken with a Super Shooter and Type 105 black and white film.

and your subject. Use a tape measure to check yourself and improve your powers of guestimation. Remember, in fairly dim light focus must be more accurate than in very bright sun. If your instant camera has a rangefinder, or you focus through the lens of an SX-70, practice with these as well.

- Pull prints from the camera with an even motion to avoid lines or tiny white dots. Lines appear if you pause. White dots occur if you pull too fast or very slowly. Pull straight—parallel to the camera body—to avoid red/yellow pressure marks or missing corners.
- Pay attention to air temperature, and use a Cold Clip for color when it's chilly or freezing.
- Consider using a shoulder bag to carry film, camera, and accessories. It can protect your camera and leave your hands free when you're shooting.

37

Looking At Light

Have you thought much about how sunlight or indoor light affects the appearance of a face or other form? Not only the brightness of light, but its direction and angle can also make the difference between a successful picture and one that is disappointing.

All kinds of daylight are ideal for instant photography. Let's look at some examples of what sunlight does to a face, since we all take pictures of people.

An example of top lighting.

1. The sun is high overhead. The model's face is clear enough, but her eyes are darkened by shadows. From this angle the sun is not flattering for portraits. This is called *top lighting,* and it is usually not good for scenics either. Mountains look rather flat in top lighting because the shadows are not very pronounced.

An example of side lighting.

2. Earlier in the day or later in the afternoon, the sun shines from a lower angle. This is called *side lighting;* it is a lot more pleasant and interesting for faces and forms. Professional photographers prefer early morning and late afternoon sunlight for scenics too, when shadows are more dramatic.

You can vary the shadow on someone's face by asking him or her to turn in different directions. If you're not sure which effect is best, shoot several variations. Side lighting is also useful for still life, because you see the form clearly.

Another type of side lighting with sun at 45-degree angle.

*An example of
back lighting.*

3. Now the sun is behind the model, a position called *back lighting.* This can be very dramatic for many subjects, but back lighting means a person's face is almost entirely in shadow. Here's how to handle that problem:

- Have the model turn slightly to one side so there is a good highlight along one edge of the face.
- Adjust the lighten/darken control of your camera toward "lighten." This will brighten shadows and give you more detail. The background may come out very light, but the person's face is more important. Shield the camera lens with your hand or a lens hood (on the Model 195 and the SX-70s), but don't block the picture area.

Using a reflector: While taking a portrait with backlight, try brightening shadows with a homemade reflector. Buy a 20x30-inch sheet of white cardboard, and have a friend hold it next to the camera, or fasten the cardboard to a wall or stand. Sunlight bounces from the reflector into shadowed areas of your subject's face, and the effect is usually flattering. You may not want to carry a reflector around with you, but at home it's a great way to get professional-looking prints. Away from home you can improvise

*Back lighted portrait
with shadows
illuminated by
cardboard reflector.*

with a newspaper or any light-colored material that's handy such as a sheet or towel.

Some instant cameras allow you to shoot flash in daylight as a way to illuminate shadows. Check your instruction booklet for this information.

Curved cardboard reflector lights the shadows of the model's face in back lighting situation.

Reflected light from a wall opposite this couple is soft and pleasant for a portrait.

Shadowless lighting: Here the couple's faces are seen almost without shadows. Reflected light is the main source. Outdoors, find a light-colored wall that reflects sunlight into a shady spot, or use a cardboard reflector to do the job. This is soft and flattering light, the kind you see all the time in good advertising and fashion pictures. People seem to glow and appear more glamorous. Do some experimenting to achieve instant prints with the subtle lighting of expensive studio-made portraits.

Judging the light: Before snapping someone wherever he or she happens to be standing, look around and analyze the light. Awareness of its direction and angle puts you in better photographic control, and your instant prints will be more pleasing. Indoors by a window or large doorway, a model may be more comfortable, and look better, than out in the sun. Many variations of daylight, other than direct sun, are available for beautiful photographs.

The key to judging any type of light is usually, how do the *shadows* look? If shadows are soft, a face is more pleasing in a print; if shadows are stronger, a scenic is usually better defined. When shadows cover important details, the subject or camera position should be moved. Outdoors you might wait until the sun shifts. If shadows crisscross or "chop up" a face or form, move to the shade, use a reflector, or try back lighting.

Smooth lighting is usually simple in appearance and does not call attention to itself. Light should come from one main direction and create shadows that define a form without being objectionable. If you have floodlights, or can borrow some, practice shooting portraits with instant black and white film. You will see how light changes as it or the subject is moved, and you can improve your prints immediately. Practice with still life as well. Place a bowl of fruit and some books on a table. Move your lights slowly and watch what happens to highlights and shadows. Snap a number of variations; later you can refer to these prints to help remember what light does from different directions and distances.

Simple still life in back lighting from the sun. It was cropped in enlarging from a Type 105 negative.

Shooting in the Shade

If you have heard the "rule," "Shoot with the sun coming over your shoulder," you realize by now that it is superficial. Sometimes the sun behind you may be fine, but it's only one possibility for good lighting.

Don't hesitate to take pictures on a hazy or cloudy day, in the shade or even in the rain. Color films produce nice warm skin colors, and black and white films have plenty of contrast without sunlight. People are comfortable in the shade, and a hazy or rainy day can help make a soft and moody landscape photograph in color or black and white.

When you take pictures of people, look for a shady spot first, preferably one with sunlight reflected into it. Under a tree, beside a house, or on a porch the light is often bright enough. If there's not enough light for a Zip or Super Shooter camera, switch to flash. The combination of flash and daylight in the background can be terrific.

The photographer used a Super Shooter in a snowstorm, knowing that the gray light would be adequate and would add to the mood of the scene. Photo by Barbara Jacobs.

Brace the camera: Some instant cameras have a threaded tripod hole in the base, and with the SX-70, you attach a tripod adaptor. When daylight is dim, you can still get sharp pictures—often quite unusual ones—by using a tripod or bracing your camera for an exposure that is too slow for a hand-held camera. From the first print you will know whether to lighten or darken, or whether you need flash. If you cannot use a tripod, set the camera on a flat rock, or a table or a box. Depress the shutter button gently and don't shake the camera. Switch to Type 107 black and white film in weak light, because it is so sensitive. In Chapter 5 there's more about how film "collects" light during longer exposures.

Light and Technique

Flare: Though back lighting is frowned upon in most camera instruction booklets, use your own judgment. By shooting "against the light," as it's called, you can get some unusual effects. Sometimes when the sun shines directly into your lens, there are flare marks on the print. These may appear as a blur or as strange shapes that you did not see in the viewfinder. To avoid these, use a lens shade or your hand above the lens.

Camera shake: Slight camera movement at the moment a picture is snapped ruins more prints than almost any other mistake. Practice depressing the shutter button gently, because if you jerk it, the camera will also be jerked. In bright light an instant camera selects a fast shutter speed, and movement is not so much of a problem; in the shade or at dusk, however, caution is very important. You will recognize camera shake if everything in a print is fuzzy and not sharp. If some areas of a picture are sharp, but the subject you wanted is fuzzy (and it wasn't in motion), your focusing distance is the problem.

45

An example of camera shake, taken after dusk when dim light caused an automatic exposure instant camera to expose for longer than the photographer could hold the camera steady.

A mixture of light: Indoors, or anywhere daylight is mixed with artificial light, black and white prints will be fine, but color prints may look strange. Ordinary light bulbs and floodlights produce warm color, especially if artificial light is stronger than daylight. Fluorescent lighting often causes annoying green and blue tones, especially on faces. In this case, switch to flash to correct the color.

Shadows and haze: On a very cloudy day or in a very shadowed area, colors may appear slightly blue in a print. Enjoy the effect when you can; if it is objectionable, try a 1A Skylight filter over the lens. Such a filter may be available to mount over your lens. If not, make your own. Buy the Skylight filter as a small square of plastic and cut it into a circle larger than the lens. Tape this over the lens to warm the occasional scene or portrait that appears in cool tones on color prints. Use a smaller circle over the electric eye, or turn

This picture is slightly underexposed; the water is very bright, so the camera exposure darkened the shadows.

the lighten/darken control to adjust for any change in the film speed caused by filtering.

You become aware of light and its many variations as you take more pictures. Be sensible and at times, be daring as well. Take pictures in lighting conditions that are not conventional. Use the lighten/darken control, and shift yourself or your model to find the best angle. There's a lot to be said for shooting "in a new light," as the saying goes. In a minute or less you will see the effects of taking chances and being creative.

By moving the lighten/darken control slightly toward "lighten," the water is not as well exposed as in the photo above, but there is more detail in the shadows.

4 Shooting with Flash

When there's not enough light for sharp pictures with an instant camera, switch to flash. Here are several ways to tell when the time is right.

- You take a picture and see that it's slightly fuzzy because you could not help moving the camera.
- Your print indicates that existing light is too weak, because people and things are too dark and indistinct.
- The print exposure is okay, but too limited an area is sharp, and everything else is out of focus.
- Exposure is satisfactory, but the print is too contrasty; this means it's bright in light areas and too dark everywhere else. The electric eye system of an instant camera tries to adjust exposure for highlights and shadows, but with too little light the shadows come out with no detail. Of course, this can be moody and effective if you like it.

Flash photography offers advantages and disadvantages. On the plus side, flash is very handy light and easy to use. It is fast enough to catch many types of action sharply, and it makes pictures possible when existing light is too dim.

On the minus side, flash lighting is flat, which means that shadows are all behind the subject, and this is not very interesting. People's faces often look fine, but light and dark effects are monotonously similar. Nevertheless, in many cases there's no substitute for flash.

Flash is fast and gives you good details in instant prints which can be corrected or improved moments after exposure.

How Light "Falls Off"

No matter where you are, the intensity of sunlight is uniform. However, this is not true of artificial light such as flash. The farther flash or floodlight must travel from the bulb, *the weaker it gets.* When photographers say "the light falls off," they mean that subjects closer to the flash will be brighter (and usually correctly exposed), while background subjects will be darker (and usually underexposed). In math terms, a subject five feet from the flash gets four times as much light as one ten feet from the flash.

Manufacturers of instant cameras are quite aware of what happens to flash as its light travels farther from the bulb. They cannot change the laws of physics, but they do design equipment cleverly to adjust itself automatically for flash exposures—*if* you focus correctly. Keep this fact in mind: Correct focus is essential for well-exposed flash pictures. Here's what to expect:

49

Light "falls off" or diminishes in brightness as it gets farther from the flash source.

1. If you focus on the person nearest the camera, that person and anyone about the same distance from the flash will be correctly exposed.

Correct focus resulted in a well-exposed flash picture.

Overexposed flash print of the same group was caused by camera being incorrectly focused a few feet behind them.

2. If you focus several feet *behind* the person nearest the camera, that person will be overexposed (too bright or washed out in the print), while people farther back will be correctly exposed.

3. If you focus a few feet *in front* of the person nearest the flash, that person will be somewhat underexposed, or darker than you wished.

4. As the distance from the flash to the nearest person or object increases, the effectiveness of flash decreases. You will find in camera instruction booklets a maximum recommended distance, such as ten feet, at which you should focus for flash when shooting color pictures. The intensity of a small flashbulb or cube is limited. Therefore, at distances greater than about ten feet, the light diminishes or "falls off" too much to provide suitable exposures on Polacolor films. The maximum distance for faster black and white films (Types 107 and 87) is closer to twenty feet. Check the instruction booklet for your camera.

51

Though the people in the second row are slightly darker than those in front, the photographer tried to get everyone about the same distance from the camera so they would be evenly lighted.

5. If you photograph a group of people, as it says in the Zip booklet, "Try to have everyone about the same distance from the camera so they'll all be lighted evenly." Otherwise, those in the middle or back rows will be darker in your print than those in front where you focused.

Flash for Specific Cameras

Flash sources vary somewhat for specific cameras, so let's examine them separately.

The Polaroid 400 series: You use a flashcube in the Polaroid Focused Flash unit which is designed for use only with General Electric Hi-Power flashcubes or their equivalent. Other flashcubes are not bright enough. When the unit is attached to a 420, 430, or 440 camera, and the cord is plugged into the proper socket, the shutter is automatically set at a constant speed. In front of the Focused Flash unit is a set of variable louvres which open and close as the cam-

Focused Flash unit for Polaroid 400 Series cameras: the louvres in front adjust automatically for correct exposure.

era is focused to adjust the intensity of light according to the distance focused. It is an ingenious system, and the working range for color is between 3½ and 10 feet from the camera.

After each flash, remember to advance the lever that turns the flashcube for the next picture. Also remember that the lighten/darken control ring around the camera lens has no effect on pictures made with flash. Instead, use the lighten/darken lever on the Focused Flash unit to open or close the louvres slightly, if a print is too dark or too light. Focus a Series 400 camera with the flash unit attached, and watch the louvres move.

The Super Shooter: Regular flashcubes or Hi-Power cubes can be used with this camera. You can shoot between four feet and eight feet with regular cubes, and up to twelve feet with Hi-Power cubes. If you move closer than four feet, prints will be overexposed, at least on close subjects.

When you insert a flashcube, wind it as far as it will go.

Flashcube rotates automatically on the Super Shooter and a plastic shield softens the light.

A spring in the socket rotates the cube as you shoot. If you insert a partially-shot cube, wind it completely, pull it out, and insert it again with a fresh bulb facing forward. Use the lighten/darken control for flash just as you would for daylight.

The Zip and Electric Zip: Above the lens of the Zip camera is a distance scale in feet. You set this at your best guess of the distance between the camera and the subject, but *only for flash.* As you turn the red exposure control knob, the same one you use in daylight, you are adjusting the lens opening of the Zip camera. In other words, if you set the distance at ten feet, the lens opening is wider than for five feet. You do not use the "YES" system for flash photography.

With the Electric Zip, you set the focusing distance on a footage scale located around the lens. The electric eye shutter handles exposure, if your focus is accurate.

Both Zip cameras include a color spot in the finder as a guide for flash. Place the color spot over a person's face, and move back and forth until the spot spans from the top of the head to the point of the chin. You will then be four feet away with the Zip and about five feet away with the Electric Zip. The color spot is not designed for use with small children or pets, and you don't have to be exactly four or five feet from a subject to take successful pictures, but it's a useful location from which to begin. You can shoot flash pictures between four and twenty feet with the Zip and AG-1 flashbulbs; with color film the limit for the Electric Zip is twelve feet with standard or Hi-Power cubes.

The Model 195: With its large lens and manually-set shutter, this is a sophisticated camera offering creative flash controls, but it is not automatic. There's a universal accessory shoe on top of the camera into which you can slip most compact standard flashguns (using several types of flashbulbs) or an electronic flash unit. Try a flashgun or flashcube adaptor on a Model 195 at a camera shop, and compare results with a small electronic flash unit.

Electronic flash, powered by batteries or a plug-in AC cord, costs more at first, but if you shoot a dozen flash shots a month, in less than a year it can save you money. Electronic flash can be fired over and over with about ten seconds of waiting between shots while the power builds up again (called recycling). There are many types and brands of electronic flash on the market, with a wide choice of prices and power. Some include a small sensor that measures light reflected from the subject and instantly quenches the light to provide correct exposure automatically. You merely set dials for film speed and lens opening on the unit, making automatic electronic flash very convenient with the Model 195 Polaroid Land camera.

Another advantage of flash with the Model 195 is that you can point the flashgun or electronic flash unit at the ceiling to bounce or reflect the light evenly over one or more subjects. Bounced light is softer and more flattering than direct flash, and light does not fall off as noticeably in group shots. Bounced light is diffused, and often preferable to direct lighting.

If you use non-automatic electronic flash or flashbulbs with a Model 195 camera, you must determine exposure by means of a *guide number.* You'll find a series of guide numbers on the carton of bulbs or cubes, or in the instruction book or on the back of an electronic flash unit. You use the guide number for the film in your instant camera, and divide it by the number of feet from flash to subject, in order to determine the f-stop for a picture situation. For instance, if the guide number for an electronic flash unit is 80 for Polacolor film, and the distance to a subject is 10 feet, 80 divided by 10 equals 8. Therefore you set the lens opening at f/8.

The SX-70s and Pronto: These cameras use a Flashbar array which has ten bulbs, five on each side of the bar. Plug the bar into the slot above the lens, *focus carefully,* and the SX-70 automatically determines the correct exposure. Slight adjustments can be made with the lighten/darken control dial. After firing five bulbs on one side of the bar,

A ten-shot Flashbar is inserted into the top of all SX-70 models, making fast sequence photographs easy.

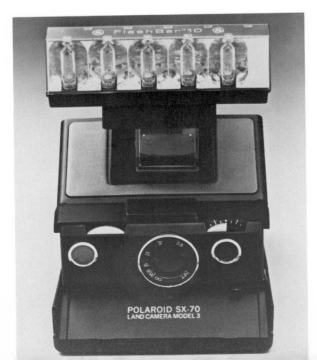

turn it around to fire the second side of five. The camera automatically fires the next good bulb facing the subject, but if all five are used, it will make an exposure anyway, without flash. You may get a time exposure for which you're not prepared, and camera movement is likely.

The flash range for SX-70 photography extends from ten inches to about twenty feet. Focused at ten inches, the lens opening is very tiny, about f/90, and the depth of sharp focus from near to distant subject is greater.

The Model 3 and Pronto operate in the same way as the Deluxe and Model 2, except that you guess the focusing distance or measure it with a tape. If your first print is not perfect, adjust your focus and try again.

Since the SX-70 is motorized, you may shoot five flash shots in quick succession. This can be handy for situations such as cutting a wedding cake or opening birthday gifts. Of course, you can shoot a rapid sequence of pictures with the SX-70 in daylight as well.

The Keystone Wizard XF 1000: Flash pictures for this instant camera are made in the same way as with the Polaroid SX-70 Model 3.

The Keystone Model 750: This camera uses the same Flashbar as the SX-70 and Wizard XF 1000. Exposure is automatic and is measured by an electric eye that sets the lens opening. The system will not use a flashbulb unless it's needed. There is also a warning light signal after each fifth shot, reminding you to rotate the Flashbar. Adjustments can be made with the lighten/darken control according to the brightness of subject or background.

Keystone Models 800 and 850: Both of these cameras include built-in electronic flash units, and the Model 850 has rechargeable batteries. Flash exposures are made at 1/1000 second, which "freezes" fast action, such as a basketball game or children running. Correct exposure is linked to the lens opening which adjusts automatically as you focus. Built-in flash can save money on bulbs or bars, but the waiting time of about ten seconds increases as batteries weaken. In addition, this type of light cannot be pointed toward the ceiling, or bounced, because it is permanently pointed forward.

Successful Flash Pictures

As instant photography has progressed, so has the ease of making instant flash pictures. Here are some pointers that may benefit you and your subjects.

- If possible, find a light-colored or medium-dark background for a pleasant contrast behind people. Avoid bright white which glares, and very dark backgrounds which may cause too much contrast.
- Ask people to stand a few feet away from the background, so the shadows behind them will not seem "pasted on." The closer anyone is to the background, the more it may reflect the light and alter exposure.

I shot this photo of myself and a friend by placing an SX-70 camera on the floor at an angle and attaching a self-timer to take the picture "no hands." Notice that the foreground is too light and the distant background ceiling is black, typical of flash lighting.

Use the lighten/darken control to correct for the brightness or darkness of walls or other backgrounds.

- Outdoors at night, and in very dark areas indoors, unless a background is reasonably close, expect it to appear black and empty. This effect can be dramatic or disappointing, depending on the situation. At night where there are no reflecting surfaces nearby, adjust the lighten/darken control toward "darken," unless your subject pretty well fills the print area.
- Bright or reflective surfaces may bounce light back to a lens, causing a "hot spot." This is especially true when you shoot into a mirror, or there's one in the background. Aim the camera at a slight angle to avoid this problem.

   People wearing glasses are a variation of the above. Ask them to tilt their heads up, down, or sideways to avoid direct reflections from flash.
- Flashcubes, bulbs, and bars operate at about 1/50 second. This is not fast enough to catch a car racing by, but you can learn to snap at *peak* action. If the subject is a basketball player, for instance, at the top of his leap in the fraction of a second before he begins to descend, the action slows and a flash shot can often "freeze" it. There's more about catching peak action in Chapter 7.
- If you have to shoot a group and cannot line everyone up at the same distance from the lens, turn the lighten /darken control slightly toward "lighten." People in the front row may be a bit overexposed, but those in back will be better illuminated. Instant photography offers a chance to correct your lighting immediately.
- At a sports event at night or in a large auditorium, you often see somebody stand and take a flash picture of the whole scene. You can understand how silly this is when you remember that the effective range of flash is only about twenty feet with fast black and white film.

59

A light-colored background provides good contrast. The subjects look off to the side to spare their eyes, and give the photo a focal point.

In such a setting, brace your camera and shoot a time exposure as an experiment (details in the next chapter).

- If people are afraid that your flash may "blind" them temporarily, suggest that they look off to the side. You can spare their eyes and still get good expressions.
- Flash may put tiny red marks in the pupils of a person's eyes in some prints. This is a reflection from blood vessels behind the retina, and can occur with any type of camera if the flashbulb is close to the lens. Ask people to look briefly at a bright light to contract the pupils just before you shoot a flash shot, and "red-eye" will be decreased.
- For extreme close-ups of objects with flash, the SX-70 is ideal. You could copy a page from this book, though you would have to read it with a magnifying glass.

Success with flash comes with experience. Keep a sharp eye on focus, contrasts of light and dark, placement of people and proper backgrounds. If it isn't easy at first, a little instant photographic practice can make it so.

Shooting
Time
Exposures

There's an old saying in photography: "If you can see it, you can take a picture of it." That's true, but it can also be tricky. Getting an image on film is one thing, and making that image clear enough to mean something is another. In this chapter we'll talk about taking pictures when there is a minimum of light with longer-than-average exposures, called *time exposures.* This is a technique for situations when you don't want to (or can't) use flash.

How Film "Collects" Light

The human eye can adjust to very dim light after a few minutes of conditioning. But there is a limit to how much the eye can see, even if we eat plenty of carrots which are supposed to improve night vision.

Photographic film and lenses are not limited in the same way. The longer a shutter is open, the more light is recorded or "collected" by the film being exposed in a camera. In addition, a lens with a larger opening such as f/3.8 (on the Model 195 Polaroid) allows more light to pass through at maximum aperture than a lens with a smaller opening such as f/8.8. Almost all the instant cameras are in the f/8 class except the Zip (f/17.5) and the Model 195.

The comparison chart of cameras in Chapter 2 shows that the maximum time for long exposures varies: one second for Polaroid Models 420 and 430, two seconds for the Super Shooter, five to twenty seconds for the Model 440, ten seconds for Keystone cameras, fourteen seconds for the SX-70, and unlimited for the Model 195 set on "B." (Time exposures are not possible with the Zip.) Even at two seconds, film can collect enough light to form an image on film that cannot be seen by the human eye.

Modern instant cameras are a delight to use for time exposures because you don't have to use a watch or clock; the exposure is automatic. The camera's electric eye determines how long a shutter should remain open, depending on the brightness of a scene and the speed rating of the film. Here are the things that influence photographic time exposures.

Speed of the film: Faster or more light-sensitive films such as Types 107 and 87 require shorter time exposures than slower films such as Polacolor and Type 105. This is why the Polaroid Model 440 operates in two shutter speed ranges. It times exposures up to five seconds with fast films, and up to twenty seconds with slow ones. If a scene calls for one second exposure on Types 107 or 87, Polacolor and Type 105 films will require about seven seconds.

Brightness of the scene: One of the tricky aspects of time exposures is judging scene brightness. Lights at night seem brighter to the eye than they are in actuality. Your best practice is to brace the camera, make an exposure, and determine the results from the print.

With fast black and white films you may be able to shoot a gym interior or a Christmas tree full of lights at shutter speeds fast enough to hand-hold the camera. The same scenes in color would require the camera to be anchored on a tripod or set firmly on a solid base. When in doubt, experiment; time exposures are often unpredictable.

Limits of the camera: From the list above or the chart in Chapter 2, you know the maximum length of time a shutter will remain open on specific instant cameras. Most of

Passing cars brightened this night scene so well that it has the appearance of daylight. It was made with a Model 180 Land camera on Type 105 film with a six-second exposure.

them give you plenty of time to record a great variety of subjects, from street scenes to indoor scenes where nothing moves. You will find that cameras offering up to ten seconds "collect" a lot more light than you might imagine. Black and white films are preferable indoors to avoid color distortion, although bizarre or unusual color may sometimes be pleasing.

If a time exposure is unsatisfactory because it's too dark or moving people or objects are too blurred, change to

Indoors at night, various instant cameras are capable of time exposures with existing light. This was taken with a Model 180 camera and Type 105 film. The model held still for eight seconds!

flash. When a scene is dimly lighted and too far away for flash to be effective, you may have to give up.

With a Polaroid Model 195, time your exposures with a watch or clock, because most exposure meters will not give you adequate guidance. The lens opening of this camera can also be adjusted. If you are buying a light meter and expect to make time exposures very often, get one with a cadmium sulfide (CdS) cell because they are more light-sensitive.

Time Exposure Techniques

- Read about shooting time exposures in the instruction booklet for your instant camera.
- Remember that the camera should be on a solid support. Otherwise nothing in the print will be sharp, even if the tones or color are okay.

- From the SX-70 booklet here is some good advice for all time exposures: "For best results, the light on the scene should be fairly even. Indoors, a bright lamp or window in the scene may 'fool' the electric eye and cause the rest of your picture to be too dark." However, if there is a lot of contrast, such as areas of light and dark in a street scene, you can try shooting anyway. Unusual pictures are rarely made by timid photographers!
- You must hold the shutter release button down for the entire time exposure on the 400 series cameras, the Super Shooter, and the Model 195. On the SX-70, however, after you press the red shutter button and hold it about a second, you can let go and the shutter stays open for the appropriate length of time by itself. The same is true of the Keystone instant cameras.

  There's a Polaroid #191 cable release for use with 400 series cameras. It allows you to make an exposure without touching the camera itself, because the cable release is attached to the shutter release. You may use a locking cable release (made for conventional cameras) with the Polaroid Model 195.
- The lighten/darken control on an instant camera can be very handy in time exposures as well as in daylight or with flash.

Unusual Effects

Moving lights, such as those in a street scene, make an interesting subject for time exposures. Patterns of light are unpredictable, and in color there are spots and streaks of light that give decorative effects. I once shot traffic from a moving bus. Since I knew I could not hold the camera steadily, I jiggled it slightly during an exposure of about four seconds, and the zigzag colored lines were delightful.

Light patterns at night can be exciting subjects. If your exposure needs to be corrected, time can be added or subtracted, based on study of the first print.

People in motion will blur and often will be unrecognizable; think of them as elements of design or composition rather than sharp figures. With this approach, you may get striking pictorial effects. Some prints you may toss away, but others you will value for being so unusual. In color particularly it is fun to play with time exposures of moving subject matter.

After you see the first print of a time exposure, you may decide that bright areas should be darkened or lightened; adjust the lighten/darken control for the next print. If colors in a print don't seem natural, think of your photo as if it were a painting and enjoy the effects you've created.

Be prepared to experiment and take chances with time exposures, when the light is dim or darkness sets in. You won't know exactly what to expect, but you'll see your prints right away, and make adjustments accordingly. No one using a conventional camera can take risks and see results as conveniently as you can through instant photography.

Another type of time exposure, made automatically in a Model 195 Land camera with Type 105 film. At dawn the exposure was several seconds. Photo by James Hartnett.

Composition: How You See Pictures

The arrangement of subject matter in a picture is called *composition.* The more harmoniously and effectively you arrange people and things in an instant print, the better your photography will be. Learning about good composition gives you control over what you shoot and how you view it in the finder. Of course, not every subject is under control. Things and people move, light changes, poor backgrounds may not be avoidable, color can be gaudy, and sometimes there is little choice of camera position. Even so, there are guidelines for good composition, and they make the difference between ordinary prints and outstanding ones.

I didn't say there were "rules" for composition, because that word is too rigid. Creativity can't be regimented. The winners in many photo contests do not please everyone, and not all photographs in a book or museum exhibit will have the same appeal to you. However, there are certain qualities that all the best photographs have in common.

Basics of Composition

The main subject: A good composition is often arranged around a main subject, but it doesn't have to be *one* person or thing. It can be a group of people or a pattern of things, such as sailboats, cars, or trees. However, there is

68

usually one shape or group of shapes that stands out over the others.

As an example, in the photo of the child feeding the pigeons, the child is obviously the main subject. In a portrait, the person's face is dominant, and the rest of the picture is secondary. In a group, all the faces are the main interest, and in a landscape the dominant form might be something in the foreground or in the distance, depending on size, color, and contrast.

As you look through the viewfinder of an instant camera, decide which element of the composition is the most important and make it the main subject. You may have to move around to create the best arrangement.

Secondary subjects: Other forms in a composition are secondary to the main subject. These elements are also important, such as the pigeons being fed by the child, but they are secondary because of their size, placement, color, emotional quality, and other things to be discussed. When you snap a picture, you may not think of secondary subjects, but you realize their value when you analyze a print.

Elements of a Composition

Composition is really good design, and the following are some of the visual elements you learn about in a design course. One or more of these may be the main and secondary subjects.

Lines: As an example, the curb behind the child feeding the pigeons is a strong line. The divisions in the pavement are secondary lines. In the picture of the riverboat at Disneyland, horizontal, vertical, and oblique lines are important to the composition, and to the boat which is the main subject. Photographers often make an arrangement of lines in a print without doing it consciously.

Shapes and forms: In a good composition you are aware of the relationships of shapes and forms to each other, and also to lines. You try to control the placement of the shapes and forms. Should the tree be in front of the window or beside it? Would Aunt Martha look better on the

Lines and textures are important elements in this Disneyland scene.

porch steps or sitting in a chair? Should the camera be higher to accent the foreground of a scenic picture, or lower to make the distant mountains more looming? How far should the shape of the riverboat come into the viewfinder for a good relationship with the background?

Forms and shapes are the main elements of composition. Lines may be part of the shapes, or they may be separate.

Texture: Most textures are on the surface of forms, and we take them for granted. But a texture may be so strong that it becomes distracting. Patterns in shirts, blouses, ties, and so on are surface textures. When there is a choice, ask people to wear fairly plain clothing for portraits.

Patterns or textures can also be the main subject or important secondary subjects. The rugged trunk of a redwood and the pattern of leaves are an example. Rows of empty

Strong textures help make a good composition.

grandstand seats might be a strong picture if the light is right and you have a good camera position. Reflections become a texture that can be fascinating. There are natural and manmade textures. Some fit into a composition very well and even invite photography. Others should be avoided if they compete with the main subject.

Color: Color is also often taken for granted just because it's there. Color can be bright and exciting, or subdued and subtle. Nature usually arranges colors in a certain harmony that looks lovely in pictures. In fact, green meadows, blue skies, or red autumn leaves inspire us to photography. However, don't ignore subdued colors, particularly on a cloudy day, because Polacolor does very well with pastels and soft light.

You cannot control the color of things, but you do have a choice about placement of colors in a composition. Look again at the picture of the child feeding the pigeons. His sweater was red, his jeans dark blue, and the rest of the scene was various shades of gray and brown, except for the flesh tones. Red, yellow, orange, and combinations of these stand out in photographs, but the cooler colors may also dominate. The amount of a color and its relationship to other colors must all be considered. Look for colorful subjects, and take advantage of quiet harmonies as well.

Color doesn't stand alone, but is part of forms, lines, and textures. The Disneyland riverboat is a series of white lines, and in the background are texture shapes of green trees and yellow umbrellas. People on the boat become a pattern of small colorful spots that the eye sees collectively. Color may also cause a particular shape to dominate a composition.

Perspective: We usually think of perspective as lines or forms going back into the distance, such as these horses becoming smaller as they get farther away. At the same time, perspective creates a feeling of *space* in a picture,

72

As the line of horses extends into the background, there is a sense of space or perspective.
Photo by Barry Jacobs.

which can be another element of composition. Deep space or perspective can be dramatic, while giving a sense of scale and distance. Shallow perspective is more intimate, such as a person in a setting with limited depth.

Impact: While impact is not a separate element of composition that you can arrange like lines or color, it is a goal of good design. Pictures with impact may include strong or subtle color, emotional expressions, dynamic lines and forms. All the elements add up to an exciting composition. Impact may also come from the story a picture has to tell of people, places, or things. If you show what's happening clearly, an instant picture has impact that is appealing to many viewers.

Guidelines to Composition

Knowing the basics I've briefly described is like learning the scales on a piano. Once you learn the notes, you're ready to play. In this case you are ready to think more carefully about composition.

Placing your subjects: Usually, it is better to compose with the main subject off center in a picture. The average person's sense of design finds centered shapes or lines less interesting than the balance created by placing a dominant form left or right, up or down, away from the center of the picture. For this reason a horizon line above or below center is preferable to splitting the picture in half.

In the snow scene I placed the figure to the right and below the center of the print. Notice how your eye tends to follow the line of rocks from the left edge toward the figure. There is a broken line of snow and foliage that leads to the figure as well. I waited for my son to reach that spot before shooting. (Contrast is also involved in this scene, and it is discussed below.)

In a square picture, try to place important elements of the composition off center to please the eye.

When you shoot square pictures on Type 87 black and white or Type 88 Polacolor and SX-70 films, it is important to place subjects off-center. A square-shaped picture tends to make a composition more *static.* That means a composition is rather dull, instead of being *dynamic.* To avoid a static arrangement, place shapes of different sizes together, be aware of movement of the eye from one form to another, and try for visual variety. Dynamic composition may mean strong contrasts, a good feeling of visual movement, or brilliant colors. Even a composition without action can be dynamic because of the shapes and placement of its elements.

Look for contrasts: There are pictorial contrasts in size, shape, color, texture, tone, human interest, and perspective. In a scenic, a huge area may be in contrast to a

Contrast of light and dark can help create an appealing instant picture.

small figure, or smooth pebbles on a beach may contrast with rough breaking waves or more distant rugged rocks. In particular, keep an eye out for light against dark, for it is always an effective contrast. This is illustrated in the photograph of Monte Carlo on the Mediterranean which was taken in late afternoon sun. White buildings stand out against dark hills, and light walls contrast with shadowed areas. Light and dark, large and small, near and far, and other contrasts can all add drama to your prints.

Backgrounds count: Jumbled backgrounds foul up as many pictures as camera movement does. Watch out for the "junk" that so often appears behind people, such as wires, poles, strange blobs of color, and other annoying forms. Move your camera or ask subjects to shift to a plainer background. When you compose a picture in the viewfinder, take care to place the main subject in a dominant spot, but be alert for lines running into someone's nose or trash cluttering other areas. Simple backgrounds are a good stage setting instead of a distraction. Luckily, instant photography gives you a second (or third) chance to make improvements immediately.

Move in closer: How many dozens of pictures have you squinted at to find a little bitty person in the distance? Be sure to stand close enough for portraits and scenes. Between four and six feet is a good distance for individuals. In addition, test your instant camera viewfinder. Set it in one place, view a scene, and take a picture. Check the print with what you see in the viewfinder. Some finders tend to show you less than the lens will include, so use the *whole* finder for composition. Be sure your eye is firmly against the viewfinder window for accuracy. With a test and a few precautions, you will not cut into heads or shoot from too far away.

When you focus at or near the closest distance an instant camera allows, keep in mind that the lens "sees" the subject slightly differently from the way you see it in the viewfinder. This is not true for the SX-70 Deluxe or Model 2, but with other instant cameras, tip the finder slightly upwards for a more accurate view of the scene or person. Check the camera instruction booklet for further details.

Simplicity: The Key to Composition

- Try to place the main subject and secondary subjects in an arrangement that "reads" quickly. This means that the story you want to tell is immediately recognizable to the viewer, backgrounds are uncluttered, and there is no doubt about your emphasis.
- What you leave out adds as much to simplicity as what you include in your prints.
- Don't try for every color in one picture, but be selective.
- Look for pleasant expressions in people pictures, and snap those moments that reveal a subject's particular characteristics.
- To avoid confused compositions, find new camera

A simple background and a flashcube, combined with a pleasant expression, add up to a good portrait.

angles, or wait around until a jumbled situation seems smoother.

- Plain walls make fine portrait backgrounds. The exception is when you want to include someone's surroundings, such as a child's play area or an adult's office. Even in this case, design your composition with care to feature the person, and make the environment secondary.
- When you have your instant pictures enlarged, you can have them *cropped.* This means that some of the picture along one or more of the edges is removed or cut off to improve the composition. Draw lines on your original print with a grease pencil to show how you want it cropped. Careful cropping adds to simplicity and pictorial impact as well.
- When a composition doesn't suit you, improve it immediately. This includes expressions, backgrounds, or action, all of which can often be improved on the spot. There's no need to wait, and more satisfaction is guaranteed as you learn better photography.

Picture Projects for Practice

Many people who own or use a camera for a while often start to think, "There's nothing much to take pictures of." I hope that sounds ridiculous to you, because it's so untrue. At home and everywhere you go, everyday activities and unusual sights are all picture targets.

In this and the next two chapters, some of these situations are illustrated, with new pointers and a few that have already been mentioned. The case histories include a variety of challenges for instant photography, typical of those you will come across.

Patterns

As noted in Chapter 6, patterns make eye-catching prints. In a crowd, look around at faces and colors. Perhaps you can shoot from your seat at an event; if not, walk around and find a better camera position. When spectators are intent on football or baseball, for instance, their expressions are fascinating. The people on the next page were watching a dolphin show. Enlargements of either color or black and white prints bring out extra details, and may be worth hanging in your personal gallery.

Patterns are everywhere, from a wheat field to chimneys to rows of fence posts. In soft light or side lighting, an ordinary subject picks up sparkle and pictorial interest.

Look for patterns of people and things that can make exciting instant pictures.

Human Interest

Many situations fall into this category, such as people playing in a park, shopkeepers talking to customers, or friends intent on doing something and not watching you. Here the father and son were involved in a game on the porch of a mountain cabin, part of which I used to frame them. The

chair in the foreground cuts into the boy's face, but adds a feeling of space as well. I could have moved the chair to see the boy's face more clearly, but might have lost the spontaneity of this human interest scene.

Sports and Action

If the setting is bright enough for black and white or color without flash, you are in luck. However, flash is often necessary to capture action indoors. If you miss the first time, try again with what you've learned.

Snap your picture when the action comes to a peak. To get this photo, I watched a whale leaping from a tank of water, and shot as it reached the peak of its motion. At this point, movement slows for a brief instant, making it easier to get sharp prints. Unfortunately, I caught the whale too close to the top of the print, but it tells the story anyway.

The camera was panned at the same speed as the passing motorcycle. Photo by Barry Jacobs.

There are several ways to shoot action sharply. Waiting for a motion to peak is one way, and *panning* the camera along with a subject moving across your line of sight is another. Here the photographer panned an instant camera to photograph a motorcycle race in a stadium after the sun had set. He used fast Type 107 film, and as the rider came opposite his seat, he estimated the focusing distance and began to swing the camera, keeping the motorcycle in the finder. When it was just opposite him, he snapped the shutter release and continued to follow through the panning movement. Since the camera was rotated at about the same speed as the motorcycle moved, the main subject is sharp, but the background is blurred. This is typical of panning. It can be an advantage because a blurred background is often less distracting than a sharply focused one. Panning a camera allows you to get a reasonably sharp print of a fast moving subject in sunlight or shade. Try it for unusual effects.

Another way to show action is to steady the camera on a tripod or other support, and shoot in fairly dim light when you know that moving people or objects will be blurred. If you photograph a street at dusk, the buildings may be sharp, but pedestrians will blur. This *suggests* action, and often results in pictures that are different and appealing.

Scenics

In a national park or close to home you will often find good landscape or seascape situations. Whenever possible, include people or animals in your scenics; without them, your pictures must have strong design or outstanding color to be successful. A scenic shot may be a huge panorama, or something much closer, such as this photograph of young people fishing on the California coast.

The hole in the rocks *frames* the main subjects for pictorial impact. Framing refers to the use of objects or dark areas at the top or sides of a picture, giving more emphasis to the central area. Shoot from under a tree for scenics, or from under a roof or a bridge. You might even aim your camera between two people in the foreground to frame a more distant scene. Framing adds a nice personal touch to instant photography.

For this framed scene I focused slightly behind the top

edge of the window rock. If I had focused exactly on the edge of the rock, the background figures might not have been sharp. Had I focused on those figures, the edges of the rock window might have been fuzzy. As a compromise to assure sharp focus in both foreground and background, I focused a little beyond the closest object of importance.

Keep this optical rule in mind for scenics or any subject: In relation to a specific point or distance of focus, sharpness is assured a greater distance *behind* that point than in front of it. In very bright light, accuracy of focus is not as crucial as in fairly dim light. For instance, with the Electric Zip and Type 87 film in sunlight, the distance scale can be left at the 5-foot setting for sharpness from 3½ feet to infinity.

Here is a theoretical set of figures for an instant camera with Polacolor film. Suppose you focus on a subject 10 feet away in bright sun. You can expect sharpness from approximately 6 feet to perhaps 50 feet away. If the film is Type 107 black and white, if you focus at 10 feet, the range of sharpness may extend from 4 feet to infinity. These are not actual figures for a specific instant camera, but they do demonstrate what to expect in general.

For scenic pictures, don't neglect shooting in black and white, even if color is more satisfying. Many of the masters of photography, such as Edward Weston and Ansel Adams, worked almost exclusively in black and white. Adams has done many beautiful scenics and details of nature with Polaroid films, especially those that offer both a print and a negative such as Type 105 and the larger Type 55 P/N.

Animals

Pets of all kinds are always favorite subjects. Be patient as you follow a pet, and wait for it to pause or play where the background is plain enough. Try to move as close as pos-

sible, especially with small animals, and you'll have larger images in your prints. I focused on this mother cat and her kittens about four feet from the lens, and used Type 107 film to be sure the whole family would be sharp. When you are close to a subject, the area of sharpness (called *depth of field*) is shallower than when you are farther away. However, with a fast film I knew my instant camera would select a smaller lens opening in this particular light by a window, and smaller openings provide greater depth of field.

Close-ups

Sharp focus and depth of field become especially important when you shoot close-ups. If a close-up lens is attach-

Close-up pictures are possible with several instant cameras, but the SX-70 is most versatile because it will focus as close as ten inches without any auxiliary lens.

ed to any camera lens, depth of field is very shallow. One way to guarantee a greater area of sharpness is to shoot close-ups in bright light, particularly with the slower films such as color or Type 105 black and white. This picture of roses was taken with an SX-70 about fifteen inches from the flowers, and I used a tripod. Even in good light, notice how the leaves in the background are out of focus just a foot or so behind the roses. This demonstrates how shallow the area of sharp focus becomes when you are close to a subject.

Remember that in bright light an instant camera selects small lens openings which result in greater depth of field. As the intensity of light decreases, the automatic exposure system chooses larger lens openings to give you good prints, which results in a reduced area of sharpness or depth of field. Though you cannot set a specific lens opening on an instant camera (except for the Polaroid Model 195), your test shots will make you more aware of the relationship between brightness of light, film speed, focusing distance, and lens opening. For maximum sharpness (which is not always necessary), use a fast black and white film, shoot in bright light or use flash, and focus at the more distant end of the close-up range rather than the closest setting.

As you will note on the chart in Chapter 10, close-up lenses are available for Polaroid Model 440 and 450 cameras, the Model 195, and the SX-70 Deluxe and Model 2. For all but the SX-70s, the kit includes one correcting lens for the finder and another that attaches over the camera lens. The lens over the finder enables you to focus within the close-up range "seen" by the attachment over the lens.

Close-up lenses for Models 440, 450, and 195 limit you to about 9 to 15 inches from a target; the SX-70 Deluxe and Model 2 may be focused to 10 inches without a close-up lens, and to within 5½ inches with one. Since you look *through* the lens of the SX-70s, these are the most accurate instant cameras for close work.

Portrait kits are also made for the 440, 450, and 195; these do not focus quite as closely as the close-up equipment, but are more suitable for people, because the closer you are to a face, the more likely it is to appear slightly distorted.

Practice taking close-ups of ordinary things such as leaves, sand patterns, a shag rug, or groups of flowers. Sometimes if you are very close, a subject loses its identity, and it becomes a guessing game to recognize it. Take close-ups also of models you build, sewing or knitting details, and collections of stamps or toy soldiers you may want to record for the future.

87

Group Portraits

Arrange people comfortably, but close enough together so you don't have to stand too far away. Talk to keep the group's attention as you snap the shutter. Or let people talk to each other if their heads are not turned too far. Group portraits take concentration and patience, but they are worth having later.

If you wish to get into a group picture with a Series 400, Model 195, Pronto, or SX-70 camera on a tripod or solid base, use a self-timer. This gadget snaps the camera shutter about ten seconds after you set it, giving you time to join other people.

This group photo is informal with a mountain background out of focus. Because of the back lighting, I adjusted the lighten/darken control slightly toward "lighten." The faces and figures are thus not lost in shadow, though the rock on which they're standing is a bit too bright.

A Story Sequence

Though you must wait a short time to *see* an instant print, you need not wait as long to *shoot* a second or third picture at the right opportunity. For instance, as someone blows out birthday candles, snap a picture; pull it from the camera, and snap another picture of reactions or of the cake being cut. Ask someone else to time print development for you, so you can concentrate on shooting a sequence of pictures. Look for action and reaction, or progressive movement, as good subjects for a short photo series.

Additional Self-Help Projects

Here's a short list of opportunities for practicing more instant photography techniques to gain more confidence in your ability.

- Make portraits of friends or family indoors with existing light, or outdoors, preferably in the shade. Vary the poses and expressions to test your skill. Some people are difficult to please.
- Shoot some flash pictures under unfamiliar circumstances, such as in a very large room or outdoors at night. The experience will guide you later in the adjustment of the lighten/darken control.
- Experiment with color photography in early morning and late afternoon when the light is warmly tinted. At midday, retreat to the shade, and study the color of prints because they may be cooler or bluer than usual.
- Set your camera on a tripod or firm base, focus carefully, choose a spot to include yourself in a scene, and take the picture with a self-timer. You may be the only individual in the print, and look quite natural walking or resting without staring at the camera.

Every new picture situation you meet can help advance your knowledge of instant photography. Exploration can mean real satisfaction and progress.

8 Picture Projects for Fun

Experience gained in the situations described in the last chapter can help prepare you for the fun and profit projects in this and the next chapter. Since instant photography is so convenient for learning camera skills, having fun and gaining confidence go hand in hand.

Party Suggestions

Unless it's an outdoor daytime party, you'll need flash. Just keep in mind that proper exposure is based on sharp focus. On some occasions you might pretend you're a reporter, and catch the action and expressions you know would interest readers of a mythical magazine. Later the prints will remind you of the music and mood everyone enjoyed.

In the photo opposite, the hostess is sharing a moment of fun with the subject of her last instant exposure. Later she can have duplicate prints made for guests, or shoot a situation more than once. Having pictures immediately is a distinct party asset that users of conventional cameras have to miss.

At your own party, be sure to ask someone to take a few pictures that include you. If you photograph a friend's party, leave some prints or have the best shots duplicated to give as a gesture of thanks.

Here are a few instant picture games for parties:

- Ask each guest to act out a phrase, as you do in charades, and give prizes to those who appear most expressive or dramatic in the instant pictures you shoot.
- Set your instant camera up with a portrait attachment, and place it the same precise distance from each subject. Photograph a series of people in color or black and white, each looking directly at the camera. With help from an assistant, cut each print into the same jigsaw puzzle pattern, with separate pieces for eyes, mouth, forehead, etc. With your assistant, in a place others can't watch, assemble portraits using one person's eyes, another's mouth, and someone else's nose.

The results are usually hilarious, and you can have a guessing game as well to identify individual features. Later you can give each guest your puzzle prints as favors.

- Let each person use the instant camera for a couple of shots of party fun, and award prizes for those voted "best in the show."

With a little imagination, you can think of other party game possibilities using an instant camera.

Artistic Expression

Whether a picture is "artistic" may be a matter of personal taste, but if you like its composition and color, chances are others will, too. I look for scenes in nature and man-made subjects that offer forms, contrasts, perspective, color, and relationships that please my eye. My goal is to mount and

hang some of these pictures, and enjoy them for their visual beauty.

The running stream is an example from my files. I was standing in the water with a Polaroid Model 195 Land camera loaded with Type 105 black and white film. It is sometimes a nuisance to carry a small tank of the chemical solution in which 105 negatives are stored, but it's often worth the effort in order to make enlargements later of my best efforts. Back home, I wash the negatives in running water and hang them to dry. If I have a good instant print, I know the negative is well exposed too.

There are many subjects with which you can express your own artistic vision, with the immediate reward of seeing a print on the spot. In color or black and white, look for pictorial challenges, and have your best pictures copied or enlarged for permanent pleasure.

Multiple Exposures

If you accidentally double-expose with an instant camera, chances are you will be annoyed at the waste of film and time. However, if you plan a double exposure, the results can be unusual and even striking. Here are a few pointers.

- Think carefully about how the images may overlap; light areas show best against dark ones in a multiple exposure.
- Set the lighten/darken control at least two marks toward "darken" to avoid overexposure. Ideally, each image should contribute half the correct exposure to the final print, and together they add up to just the right tonality or color.
- Look for shapes and textures that will harmonize when overlapped, but *take chances!*

It is easier to make a multiple exposure with an instant camera than almost any other way, and you can reshoot al-

Intentional double exposures are easy with instant cameras. Plan the overlap of images carefully, and set the lighten/darken control toward "darken" to avoid overexposure.

most immediately to improve your efforts. These are one-of-a-kind photographs that can be exciting to show.

Humor

Really amusing situations are not so easy to find. They happen when you're not ready, or they just aren't that funny. I liked the picture on page 95 of a mock fight, taken with a Zip camera and Type 87 film. The boys had fun, and the photographer was able to get several humorous prints. He shot a pack of eight prints rather quickly, but had the advantage of checking each one and suggesting improvements to his actors as he went along.

This posed photo was enjoyed seconds after exposure. Photo by Kevin Steck.

Still Life

Painters make arrangements of fruit, bottles, and other objects, and there are many famous still life pictures. As an exercise in lighting and composition, setting up and shooting a still life is an enjoyable way to use instant photography. Plan to shoot outdoors or by a window, unless you have floodlights available. I chose early morning sun for the arrangement of fruit and the textured glass. A sheet of gray paper covered a low table, and black cardboard gave the picture contrast while it covered the distracting wall behind it. With a close-up lens on a Polaroid Model

180 camera, I used a tripod and focused on the stem of the glass about a third of the way into the composition. In order to assure complete sharpness, I set the f-stop at f/45 to give me depth of field similar to that which an automatic camera offers. This is another advantage of instant cameras, because conventional equipment does not include such small lens openings.

Pictures at School

In addition to photography for a school newspaper, discussed in the next chapter, several other fun projects are possible. For instance, you might document a class activity or play as it progresses. Shoot rehearsals of a play as a record, and your prints may aid the actors by showing them the impression they are making on stage. If you are in the play or part of the classroom activity, set the camera on a tripod, compose the pictures, and ask someone to snap them for you; or use a self-timer. When friends or relatives are graduating, take your instant camera to the ceremony, and make some portraits in cap and gown as gifts. You might offer your photographic services to a teacher in whose class something is happening that would benefit from color or black and white prints.

The Family Album

Instant photography gives us all the opportunity to see pictures of everyday life, of vacation trips, and of all our activities, just moments after they are taken. People get a lot of satisfaction at the time, even if they may be critical of how you caught their expressions or poses. You can build a valuable collection of images that are irreplaceable in the future. The best of these should be included in a photo album. In Chapter 11 there are descriptions of albums for instant prints, and ways of taking care of them.

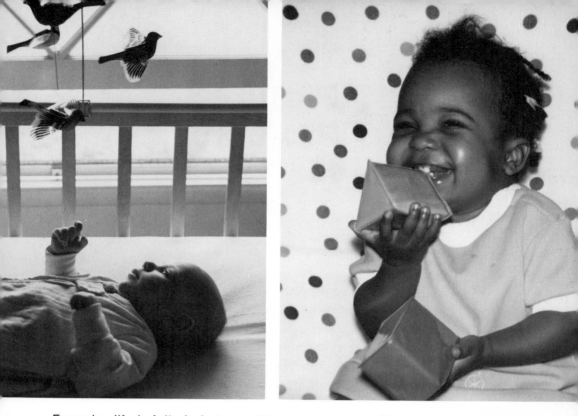

Everyday life is full of photographic moments that will be valued in a family album years later.

Among the situations you might consider in such an informal pictorial record are pictures of visitors, your hobbies, club meetings, people at work, moving day, holiday celebrations, and even sad occasions as well as happy ones. Lots of things that may not seem important now will remind you of people and places years later. Younger children enjoy seeing images of where the family lived and how their brothers and sisters looked before they were born. Even casual scenes of personal history will seem more significant as a family album grows and changes occur.

Carry your camera to places where you may not have taken pictures before, as well as to the usual ones. The reward for being alert is the pride of taking better photographs that help to enrich your life.

97

9 Picture Projects for Profit

As your instant photography really improves, you may find opportunities to shoot pictures for pay. At the same time, you may think of ways to sell instant prints, duplicate prints, and enlargements. Of course, there are professional photographers in every community. But many photographic jobs that are too small for a professional can be tackled by a competent amateur.

You can offer a personal photographic service to friends, family, and organizations. Your clear, sharp prints in daylight or with flash can be sold on a basis that seems fair to you and the buyer. Take into account how many pictures are needed and how long it will take to shoot them. Ask the buyer how much he or she is willing to pay for each picture or for the whole job. If the total does not amount to enough per picture or per hour to suit you, suggest your own rate. Be sure to figure out the cost of materials, such as film and flash. Extras such as enlargements should be charged for separately.

While selling your services, remember to tell buyers that enlargements or duplicate prints are easily available, because a lot of people still think of instant prints as one-of-a-kind. If you can shoot Type 105 black and white film, having a negative for later use is often a big selling point to buyers. You or your client can order prints of excellent quality from Type 105 negatives. With a home darkroom, they could really make your hobby pay off.

Here are some suggestions for picture projects for profit.

Parties and Weddings

It's not difficult to take pictures for the host or hostess while you're a guest at a party or wedding. Keep a supply of flash-cubes, bulbs, or bars handy along with enough film. Make a list of people and situations your employer wants to be sure are photographed, especially close friends and family members. Roam about looking for people having a good time, dancing, playing games, or conversing.

Estimate with your employer about how many pictures he or she expects, and take time to relax between shots. Suggest an album of the party or wedding, if it's big enough. Someone else might help you by taking orders from guests for duplicate prints which you can deliver later, perhaps by mail.

If you are asked to take pictures in a church during a wedding, check beforehand for permission. Flash may not be allowed, so exposures will be very slow. Use fast black and white film (Types 107 and 87), because you will get

Prints of this couple having fun at a party were sold to them as well as to the hostess for her own album.

blurry, warm-toned color pictures indoors with time exposures.

At a social event, when you are hired, try to avoid showing your prints as they are taken. It takes up time, and some of your pictures may disappear as well. Instead, plan a display of pictures at the end of the event. Number all the prints and then take orders.

Community Service

This category includes pictures of fund-raising events, instances of pollution, speakers at meetings, visiting VIPs, and many other subjects that people want to have photographed. A neighborhood newspaper may welcome your services, pay your expenses, and pay for prints they use. This experience is excellent. Subjects such as neighborhood Christmas decorations, new playgrounds, people who have won recognition for achievement, and service club activities are among those you might suggest to local editors. In some cases you may want to donate your time if an organization or company pays for film and flash. Remind clients that you can provide enlargements for display or publicity, and charge extra for additional prints.

This photo of tangled brush helped an environmental group show how negligence was ruining the landscape near a housing development.

Real Estate

Many real estate dealers use their own instant cameras to photograph homes and other property for sale or rent. You might offer to help a busy broker save time by shooting such pictures on a regular basis at a fee per shot or per hour. Remember to use a cloud filter for black and white prints; a wide-angle lens attachment may also be handy (see Chapter 10). Your skill counts in this kind of job, because dealers may not handle an instant camera as well as you do.

School Newspapers

Instant black and white prints or conventional enlargements made from Type 105 film are both appropriate for school newspapers. As you photograph classroom activi-

News events, such as a visiting musical group, can be photographed to meet fast deadlines for a school newspaper.

ties, visiting speakers, sports, or whatever is news, you'll know right away if exposures and expressions are okay. (Don't get distracted showing off your prints and forget your picture-taking!)

Newspaper printers are usually happy to work with original instant prints that have good contrast. If not, plan to have enlargements made quickly; Type 105 negatives are a big advantage here. For a few shots of a situation, an instant camera can compete very nicely with a conventional one, and you can deliver to the editor in a few minutes. For this type of work the versatility of a Polaroid Model 195 camera (or the older Model 180) is great.

Owners and Collectors

Good pictures are always welcome to the owners or collectors of cars, boats, planes, coins, etc. Check local newspapers for shows and meetings where people proudly display antiques or sports equipment. Many exhibitors could be ready customers for instant photography. Though you may be a stranger, it's easy to demonstrate your photographic skill in a few minutes.

Service to Small Business

This list here is endless. Creative people often want photographs of their handiwork, such as weavings, paintings, or pottery. Businessmen may want a record of new displays, signs, or remodeling. Builders need pictures showing the progress of a home or office building as it is constructed. Bakers could use pictures of special cakes to show future customers. Small companies might hire you to shoot new products or processes for company newsletters. Merchants selling many kinds of items may be happy to have instant prints to send to mail-order customers, if they real-

The owner of this bookstore wanted pictures of special displays.

ize you are available. Let it be known that you "have camera, will travel."

Children and Neighbors

While many families have their own cameras, parents are often too busy to use them, and the idea of instant prints is intriguing. Therefore, you may have a market for informal shots of children at play or posed. As a start, make a small sample album (give duplicates to the family you use as models) to show around the neighborhood. Many parents will be happy to pay you to take pictures while they hold babies or distract small children. Photographing children's birthday parties could also become a specialty that helps to build your reputation.

Because prints do not have to be timed during development, and there are no negatives to discard, the SX-70 is ideal for photographing children. Remember to leave order blanks, so people can have their own duplicates or enlargements made. If the family owns an instant camera that is better than yours, offer to use it to improve your results.

Publications and Contests

Your personal prints with outstanding artistic value may also be worth money. Some magazines devoted to photography accept and pay for pictures from unknown contributors. Composition, color, and subject matter must be unusual or exciting because there's so much competition, but if you're talented don't hide it. Check the library or newsstands for potential photo magazine markets, and evaluate what they use. Choose pictures with care, and have duplicates made before you send originals. Enlargements of your most impressive pictures are advisable; if they are not accepted by a publication or contest, hang them on your own walls.

Send a stamped, self-addressed envelope to assure return of your prints. Include a few caption notes to increase an editor's interest. It takes artistry and an individual touch to shoot topnotch photographs, and as yours improve, you may as well try for fame and fortune.

Photos taken for their special color, composition, or subject matter can be submitted to publications and contests.

*A community group's pet show offers great
photo possibilities.*

Other Possibilities

Here are a few additional ways to make money through instant photography.

- Cover a pet show and sell prints to owners of dogs, cats, etc.
- Attend a local talent show and offer prints to contestants or promoters.
- Keep track of community programs such as plays, dance performances, operettas, and musical groups; check with those in charge and offer to take pictures for a reasonable price.
- Once you have a business routine underway, have a business card printed that people can refer to after you contact them.

These suggestions will help you think of more in your own neighborhood. People are still fascinated by instant photography, even though it has been around for many years. Your clients will be amazed at the high quality of color or black and white prints. With imagination and persistence, your hobby can more than support itself.

Accessories for Instant Cameras

An accessory is any attachment or piece of equipment that did not come with the instant camera originally. Many accessories make it possible to shoot a wider variety of pictures, including unusual effects.

Carrying Cases and Shoulder Bags

A case for your camera helps to protect it. If the case has a hand or shoulder strap, it also makes carrying the camera easier. There are no snug-fitting cases for some instant camera models, but that may not be a handicap. A shoulder case with compartments inside is very convenient for camera, film, flash, and print storage until you get home. Here is a list of cases for current Polaroid Land cameras.

CAMERA MODEL	TYPES OF CASES
420 430 440 450	Carrying cases #476 and #477 hold camera, extra film, flash unit, cubes, etc. #477 is the larger of these, and shoulder straps come with each.
Model 195	Use a conventional gadget bag with shoulder strap; choose a convenient size for camera and accessories.

Snug-fitting case for the SX-70 has a neckstrap and fold-down front flap for easy access to the camera.

CAMERA MODEL	TYPES OF CASES
Super Shooter & Super Shooter Plus	Snug-fitting case is #411.
Zip	Snug-fitting case is #2010.
SX-70 (2 models)	Leather camera carrying case #114; leather Eveready case with shoulder strap #122; compartment case for camera and accessories #116.

Note: For older model Polaroid Land cameras, case numbers are: Colorpak, #342; Square Shooter, #342, #411; Model 180, #328; Swinger, #320.

In addition, many sizes and shapes of conventional shoulder or gadget bags can be adapted for instant cameras. I prefer a shoulder bag to a snug-fitting case, because it leaves my hands free to shoot, and I don't have to put the bag down where it may be forgotten or stolen.

107

Four compartmented carrying cases for various Polaroid instant cameras, all of which come with a shoulder strap.

Portrait and Close-up Lenses

These are handy accessories for instant cameras. You can get closer to people and fill more of the print, and you can shoot small objects more efficiently. Here's a lineup of attachments for Polaroid Land cameras.

CAMERA	LENS KITS
420 430 440 450	Kits not available for Models 420 and 430; Portrait Kit #541 and Close-up Kit #543 for Model 440; Portrait Kit #561 and Close-up Kit #563 for Model 450. These kits consist of a clip-on view/focus adaptor, an accessory lens, and a flash diffuser (to decrease flash intensity because you're so close to a subject). With a Portrait lens you can shoot as close as 19 inches for head and shoulder portraits. With a Close-up lens you can work as close as 9 inches for small objects.

A portrait lens slips neatly over the camera lens, and a correction lens fits over the viewfinder.

CAMERA	LENS KITS
Model 195	Portrait Kit #1952 and Close-up Kit #1951.
Super Shooter Zip	No lenses or kits available.
SX-70/Deluxe & Model 2	Close-up Lens #121 used with Accessory Holder #113; flash diffuser for close-ups.

Filters and Other Accessories

Here's more equipment to expand your picture-taking possibilities. All are for Polaroid Land cameras, and you can ask to try one or more of these before you buy. The same advice applies to a lens kit. Take a few pictures in or near the shop, and see if you like the results.

CAMERA	ACCESSORIES
420 430 440 450	Development timer #128 for Model 420; cable release #191 and self-timer #192 for all models; UV (ultraviolet) filter #585 and cloud filter #516 for all models *except* 420.
Model 195	Cable release #191, orange filter (in #595 filter kit), lens shade (with filter kit), 5S light-reducing filter.
SX-70 (all models)	Tripod mount #111, remote shutter button (18-inch cable) #112, accessory holder #113, lens shade #120, self-timer #132.
Pronto	Accessory kit: cable release, self-timer, accessory adapter, and tripod adapter.

Filters: An ultraviolet (UV) filter reduces excessive blue in shadows outdoors, and is useful at high altitudes or for distant mountain scenes. The UV filter is colorless and helps protect the lens if you leave it in place all the time.

A cloud filter is orange and helps darken skies in black and white pictures *only,* making clouds show up with more contrast. If you use a colored filter with Polacolor film, you will tint the whole print, which might be annoying or a nice offbeat effect, depending on the subject. These filters have no effect on gray skies, haze, fog, or rain.

Filters are made with an extension that covers the electric eye of a 400 Series camera, and automatic exposures are made in the normal way. Since the filter diminishes light intensity slightly, the camera chooses a larger lens opening than it would without a filter. Depth of field may be affected, but in bright light, no change of sharpness should be noticeable with fast Types 107 and 87 film.

An orange cloud filter helped darken the sky behind these flowers.

The 5S light-reducing filter for the Model 195 is gray, has no effect on color, cuts light intensity about five stops or lens openings, and is often called a neutral density filter. With very fast film especially, the photographer has a wider choice of lens openings and shutter speeds with the Model 195, using the 5S filter. It can also be useful with flash when you are fairly close to a subject. The 5S filter may help prevent overexposure, and can be used with any type of film.

Cable release: For time exposures, when you don't want to touch the shutter release directly and risk shaking the camera, a cable release is the answer. It screws into the shutter release button of all but the Super Shooter and Zip cameras.

Self-timer: When your camera is on a tripod or other solid base, with a self-timer you have about 10 seconds (after pressing the shutter button) to get into the picture yourself. This is useful when you want to be included in a group. When you shoot a scene in which you want a person, and there's nobody around, use a self-timer, dash 20 or 30 feet into the picture, and pose candidly as if the camera were not there!

For slow exposures, especially when your camera is braced, use a self-timer instead of a cable release if you wish. It's a no-hands operation.

111

Self-timer for SX-70 fits over the shutter release button and activates it after a ten-second delay.

Batteries

Battery power activates instant camera shutters and flash as well, so these small units of electricity are hardly accessories. However, there are many battery look-alikes that will not work in your camera. Be certain you use the correct number and type.

Other Accessories

As a substitute for changing lenses on some instant cameras, Kalimar, Inc. manufactures add-on lenses for certain older models in Series 100, 200, and 300 by Polaroid, as

Kalimar kit consists of telephoto (on camera) and wide-angle auxiliary lenses, plus finder attachment which is adjustable.

well as the current Polaroid 400 Series. Here are brief descriptions.

Auxiliary telephoto lens: It screws onto the lens of a Series 400 camera, producing a magnification of about twice the normal image size. This means if you shoot a scene from fifty feet with the telephoto lens, the print will look as though it were taken from about twenty-five feet away. To see what the lens is doing, you attach a Kalimar finder on top of the camera's finder, and use it to compose your picture. This auxiliary finder is adjustable for use with the wide-angle lens as well.

Auxiliary wide-angle lens: This also screws onto the lens of a Series 400 camera, increasing the area covered by about 75 percent. For example, if you shoot a scene from fifty feet away, the wide-angle lens produces an image similar to one taken from about eighty-seven feet away. When you're in a crowded spot and cannot move back, the wide-angle is useful. It also gives you somewhat exaggerated perspective which can be pictorially effective—or annoying.

Kalimar auxiliary lenses come in a kit with pouch, and I suggest testing them on your camera before you buy. Add-on lenses tend to reduce image sharpness slightly, but the

For an interior shot, a wide-angle lens attachment can include more of the room in the print.

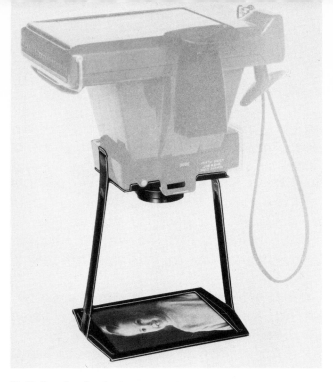

*Kali-Copier includes camera support
and close-up lens set for a specific distance
to copy instant prints quickly.*

difference is quite acceptable if a telephoto or wide-angle lens increases the fun you have with a camera.

Kali-Copier and light: For those who want to make duplicate prints at home, Kalimar makes a small camera stand with built-in close-up lens. This copier is adaptable to many instant camera models, and exposure is automatic. Copy prints, especially color, in daylight. However, if you need to copy after dark, the company makes a pair of color-corrected lights for the Kali-Copier. Check at a camera shop, and read the instructions for full details.

Miscellaneous: For experimental photography, there are other special effect filters, star filters, multiple image filters, and even fog filters made for conventional cameras. With imagination and a little effort to attach them, these may widen the scope of your picture-taking.

 Print Care and Picture Pointers

Better photographic technique includes taking care of instant prints after they are developed. Too often snapshots are stored in drawers, shoeboxes, or odd places around the house. Finding a particular photo can be a chore, if it hasn't mysteriously disappeared. These hazards can be avoided if you place your best prints in albums, and file the rest in large envelopes with labels and dates. Here's a useful system.

- Date each print. It's nice to know when your sister climbed that tree in Yosemite, or when a certain party was held. To write on the back of some Polaroid prints, use a grease pencil or buy a "Stabilo" marking pencil in a stationery store. It writes on anything, even glass.
- Shop for albums at camera stores or stationery stores. Polaroid Corporation makes two albums for instant prints. Album #519 holds seventy-two prints, either color or black and white. The larger Deluxe #521 has an expandable metal binder. Prints slip under plastic mounts back to back and you can date them on the bottom white margin if you wish.

   The Holson Company of Wilton, Connecticut makes an album called the #115 especially for SX-70 prints. They call it an "instant replay" photo album, and it holds fifty-six pictures that slip into window slots.

The album expands for more pages sold in refill packets. There's a space under each print for date and description.

Conventional albums with lift-up plastic pages are also fine for instant prints. Whatever type of album you use, take the time to fill it carefully. Protected pictures last, and are easy to find later.

- *Don't* cement prints into an album, because many adhesives include chemicals that will eventually fade or damage prints. If you must fasten prints to a surface, use transparent tape along the edges.
- Try not to mix loose instant prints with conventional photos when you store them, because chemicals left in the latter could stain or fade your instant pictures. It's okay to mount instant prints along with conventional ones in an album if they do not touch each other.

Copies and Display

Each pack of Polaroid Land film comes with an order blank for copies and enlargements. If you cannot find a blank, ask your photo dealer, or contact the nearest Polaroid office listed on the film instruction sheet.

Polaroid Copy Service makes sharp, clear duplicates and enlargements. To mat or frame a print, ask advice from a local shop unless you already know how from experience.

Film pack frame: An empty metal film pack container can be used as a handy print frame. Slide the back off, lift the inside plate, and insert a print to be seen through the window side. Position the print evenly, replace the inside plate and hold it carefully as you slide the back cover on. You will have to lift the metal cover at the end to slide the back on completely.

A pack frame will stand on end vertically, and horizontally as well if you fasten a thin piece of cardboard on the

An empty film pack is easily adapted as an instant picture frame.

bottom edge to make it level. You can also mount a pack frame on the wall with double-sided tape or a few small nails. Nail heads slip into cutouts on the back of the frame.

You might experiment with spray painting film pack frames in decorative colors. Mailing a print in a pack frame protects it, and inside you could include a cassette tape of your voice for an original gift to friends or relatives.

Display care: Sunlight fades the colors in photographic prints over a period of time, so avoid hanging them where they get direct rays daily. Even indirect sunshine will eventually fade a color print, though modern technology is constantly trying to make dyes more permanent. A color print carried in a wallet or purse, or stored in an album, should last indefinitely.

Slides: Polaroid Copy Service also makes slides in 2x2 inch mounts from any instant print. This means you can include instant pictures in a family slide showing. This option makes instant photography even more versatile.

Individual frames: Dealers sell small individual folders for instant prints, and they are handy as gifts or for display. At Christmas time Polaroid Copy Service offers multiple print copies that you can use as Christmas cards. Shoot a good family picture, include yourself with a self-timer (or have a friend take it), and enjoy sending a personalized greeting.

Final Picture Pointers

Camera instruction booklets include lists of trouble-shooting tips which you should know. A few are reviewed here because they are most important.

- Keep camera rollers clean. Even if you are in a rush to change film packs, take a moment to wipe the rollers with a handkerchief or piece of facial tissue.
- Hold the camera steadily, take a breath, and shoot. If prints are not sharp, brace the camera or use a tripod.
- Keep backgrounds simple by moving yourself or the subject. A little extra time pays dividends in better pictures.
- When shooting with flash, try to arrange people at a fairly uniform distance from the camera for even lighting.
- In all pictures, and scenics especially, don't try to include too much. You may just see a jumble, and details will be lost. Find a center of interest or main subject, avoid splitting the composition in equal halves, and if in doubt, shoot both a horizontal and a vertical picture.
- Keep your camera and lens clean. Blow or brush out dirt, sand, and smudges.

An abstract photograph I chose for display on my den wall because of its subtle relationship of colors and unusual design. It hangs out of direct sunlight which can fade color prints.

Every instant camera is made to give you satisfaction for a long time. Treat your camera like a precision instrument, and you'll have more prints that you really care about. Instant photography means images from which you can learn, be creative, and express yourself, all in seconds.

Good shooting!

Glossary

Aperture - The f-stop or opening of a lens through which light passes. The size of the aperture is adjustable according to the intensity of the light and the speed of the film.

Automatic camera - A camera with a built-in exposure meter that automatically adjusts the lens opening, shutter speed, or both, for proper exposure.

Coating - The spreading of chemicals on an instant black and white print to preserve and protect it.

Cold clip - Two sheets of hinged metal in which instant color prints are placed to warm them during development in cold temperatures.

Contrast - The brightness range of a scene or subject, from darkest shadows to brilliant highlights as recorded in an instant print.

Cropping - Removing part of an image along one or more sides to improve composition.

Depth of field - The area or distance between the nearest and farthest objects that appears in acceptably sharp focus in a photograph. Depth of field depends on the lens opening, the specific lens on a camera, and the focus setting for the distance from the lens to the object.

Electric eye - A light-sensitive cell in a camera that helps to translate light intensity to the exposure meter to achieve automatic lens and shutter operation.

Electronic flash - A compact, repeating light source for photography, powered by batteries or AC current. This flash is very fast, and can be adapted to specific instant cameras only.

Exposure meter - A separate instrument or a component of an automatic camera that measures light intensity to determine proper photographic exposure.

Film speed - The sensitivity of a specific film to light, indicated by a number such as 75 or 3,000. The higher the number, the more sensitive, or "faster," the film.

Films, pack - Instant films contained in a flat pack, either black and white or color.

Films, roll - Instant films in rolls for older models of instant cameras, black and white only.

Filter - Tinted or clear glass or plastic placed over the lens of a camera to emphasize or change the color or tonality of a scene, or of certain elements in a scene.

Flash - A brief, intense burst of light produced by a flashcube or bulb, or by an electronic unit. Flash is used when the lighting of a scene or subject is not adequate for taking pictures.

Floodlight - A special type of light bulb, usually used in a reflector, for indoor photography. Floodlights are manufactured in various shapes, sizes, and wattage ratings.

Focus - The adjustment of the distance setting of a camera lens so that a specific subject will appear sharp on film.

F-stop - A number used to indicate a precise aperture or lens opening; low f-stop numbers represent large apertures, and high f-stop numbers are for small apertures.

Lens - One or more pieces of optical glass or molded plastic designed to collect and focus rays of light to form a sharp image on film.

Overexposure - A condition in which too much light reaches the film, producing a "washed-out" instant print with inadequate contrast.

Panning - Moving a camera so that the image of a moving object remains in the same relative position in the viewfinder as the picture is taken. The main subject is sharp in the print, while the background is blurred.

Peak action - The moment when a motion comes to an apex or peak, and begins to return to its original position. At this moment it is easier to photograph action and assure sharpness as well as pictorial impact.

Rangefinder - A device used on a camera as an aid to focusing.

Shutter - The mechanism within a camera that opens and closes for an interval to allow light to expose the film. Shutter speeds are measured in fractions of a second.

Slide - A color photograph, also called a transparency, which is mounted for projection on a screen.

Time exposure - A relatively long exposure period, usually in terms of seconds or minutes, used in situations where light intensity is very dim, and for night photography.

Underexposure - A condition in which too little light reaches the film, producing an instant print that is too dark and lacks sufficient detail.

Viewfinder - The window in a camera through which you view a scene while taking pictures.

Suggested Reading List

Note: Some of these books and magazines are devoted to photography in general, but will prove helpful to users of instant cameras.

Adams, Ansel. *Singular Images.* Morgan & Morgan, Inc., 1974. A collection of beautiful photographs made on instant film materials.

Jacobs, Lou, Jr. *Basic Guide to Photography.* Peterson Publishing Co., 1973.

— *You and Your Camera.* Lothrop, Lee & Shepard Co., 1971.

Kemp, Weston D. *How to Take Better Polaroid Pictures.* Prentice-Hall, Inc., 1975.

Lahue, Kalton C. *Polaroid Photography.* Peterson Publishing Co., 1974.

Meiselas, Susan. *Learn to See.* The Polaroid Foundation, 1974. A sourcebook of 101 photography projects by teachers and students.

Pucell, Rosamond Wolff. *A Matter of Time.* David R. Godine Publisher, 1975. A picture book of instant photography.

Invitation to Photography. Published twice a year by *Popular Photography* magazine, with occasional articles on instant photography.

List of
Service
Centers

Polaroid Service Centers

Polaroid toll-free hot line: 800-225-1384

CALIFORNIA
875 Stanton Road
Burlingame 94010
(415) 692-1027

2040 East Maple Avenue
El Segundo 90245
(213) 322-6206

GEORGIA
3720 Browns Mill Road, S.E.
Atlanta 30315
(404) 762-1711

ILLINOIS
2020 Swift Drive
Oak Brook 60521
(312) 654-5252

MASSACHUSETTS
89 Second Avenue
Waltham 02154
(617) 890-7000, ext. 2924

NEW JERSEY
W-95 Century Road
Paramus 07652
(201) 265-6900

OHIO
4640 Manufacturing Road
Cleveland 44135
(216) 267-7600

TEXAS
9029 Governors Row
Dallas 75247
(214) 631-9500

Independent service facilities in many parts of the country are authorized to repair Polaroid cameras. You can call Polaroid's toll-free number to find out which one is nearest to your home.

Keystone Service Centers

CALIFORNIA
  3398 East 70th Street
  Long Beach 90805

NEW JERSEY
  Keystone Division of
  Berkey Photo
  Paramus 07652

ILLINOIS
  1555 Louis Avenue
  Elk Grove Village 60007

Index